Everyman's Poetry

Everyman, I will go with thee,
and be thy guide

Rudyard Kipling

Selected and edited by JAN HEWITT

University of Teesside

EVERYMAN
J. M. Dent · London

This edition first published by Everyman Paperbacks in 1998
Selection, introduction and other critical apparatus
© J. M. Dent 1997

7 9 10 8

J.M.Dent
Orion Publishing Group
Orion House
5 Upper St Martin's Lane
London WC2H 9EA

An Hachette Livre UK company

Typeset by Deltatype Ltd, Birkenhead, Merseyside
Printed in Great Britain by
Clays Ltd, St Ives plc

British Library Cataloguing-in-Publication Data
is available upon request.

ISBN 978-0-4608-7941-5

The Orion Publishing Group's policy is to use papers that
are natural, renewable and recyclable products and
made from wood grown in sustainable forests. The logging
and manufacturing processes are expected to conform to
the environmental regulations of the country of origin.

Contents

Note on the Author and Editor

RUDYARD KIPLING was born 30 December, 1865, in Bombay, India to Alice (née Macdonald) and John Lockwood Kipling, a professor of Architectural Sculpture at the Bombay School of Art. His early life was spent first in India, then fostered, unhappily, by a couple in Southsea, England. He was not removed from them until 1877. A year later he entered the United Services College in Devon, which was eventually to provide the background for *Stalky & Co.* (1899), and there he began to write poetry and to edit the college newspaper. Returning to India to work as assistant editor on the *Civil and Military Gazette* in Lahore in 1882, and its associated paper the *Pioneer* in Allahabad in 1887, his poems and tales, in particular *Departmental Ditties* (1886) and *Plain Tales from the Hills* (1888) brought him early acclaim. Wider literary celebrity came with Kipling's return to England in 1889 and the publication of *Barrack-Room Ballads* (1892), where his innovatory experiments with the dialect rhythms and voices of the ordinary soldier justify descriptions of him as a modern poet, and have been admired and emulated by poets as diverse as Bertolt Brecht and T. S. Eliot. Throughout the 1890s he wrote prodigiously, though it was not until *Kim* (1901) that he had any success with the longer novel form. He travelled widely, saw action in the Boer War, and was on close terms with high imperialist politicians such as Cecil Rhodes.

Critical reception of Kipling's work became increasingly divided as, from the period of the Boer War onwards, anti-imperial sentiment grew. Because of this, and despite being awarded the Nobel Prize for literature in 1907, Kipling was never to recover the acclaim awarded to him in his early years. His personal life also had its tragedies. In 1899 his daughter Josephine died from whooping cough while visiting New York, and Kipling almost died of pneumonia. The loss too of his only son, John, killed in action with the Irish Guards in 1915, helped to darken the vision of his later writing. Throughout his life he continued to experiment, particularly with the juxtaposition of prose and verse which has added to the elliptical and elusive quality of some of his best short stories, in the process building a body of verse from which a number of individual poems have taken on a public life of their own. Despite his diminished critical reputation, Kipling's work retained a popular appeal which outlasted his death in January 1936 to make him probably the last public poet of our age.

JAN HEWITT is a senior lecturer in English and cultural studies at the University of Teesside. She has written on the work of Mary Braddon and D. H. Lawrence and writes on British regional and colonial literature.

Chronology of Kipling's Life

Year	Age	Life
1865		Joseph Rudyard Kipling born in Bombay (30 Dec)
1868	3	Sister Alice (Trix) born
1871–7	6–12	Both children left with Captain and Mrs Holloway at Lorne Lodge, Southsea, 'The House of Desolation' – while their parents return to India.
1875	10	Father becomes director of the Mayo School of Art and curator of the Lahore museum
1877	12	Mother returns to England and removes the children from Southsea
1878–82	13–17	Enters United Services College, Westward Ho, Devon
1880	15	Falls in love with Florence Garrard, to whom he later becomes engaged
1881	16	Becomes editor of *United Services College Chronicle*; *Schoolboy Lyrics* privately printed by parents in Lahore
1882	17	Leaves school, arrives in India to take on post of assistant editor of *Civil and Military Gazette* in Lahore

Chronology of his Times

Year	Literary Context	Historical Events
1865	Arnold, *Essays in Criticism* Carroll, *Alice in Wonderland* Yeats born	Abraham Lincoln assassinated
1868	Browning, *The Ring and the Book* Collins, *The Moonstone*	Gladstone becomes Prime Minister
1871	Darwin, *The Descent of Man* Eliot, *Middlemarch*	Livingstone and Stanley meet on shores of Lake Tanganyika; Paris Commune
1875	Mark Twain, *The Adventures of Tom Sawyer*	Britain buys shares in Suez Canal
1877		'Empress of India' added to Queen Victoria's title; Britain annexes the Transvaal
1878	Gilbert and Sullivan, *HMS Pinafore* Hardy, *The Return of The Native* Edward Thomas born	General Booth founds the Salvation Army; Congress of Berlin; war in Afghanistan
1880	*Tit-Bits* inaugurates new style of narrative journalism for popular readership	Boer uprising in Transvaal agreement that Britain should control Afghan foreign relations
1881	Hardy, *A Laodicean* James, *Portrait of a Lady*	Pretoria Convention recognises independence of Transvaal subject to British suzerainty; Panama Canal begun; death of Disraeli
1882		Married Women's Property Act

Year	Age	Life
1884	19	Florence Garrard breaks engagement; *Echoes* produced by Rudyard and Trix
1886	21	Becomes a Freemason in Lahore; *Departmental Ditties*
1887	22	Transfers to staff of the *Pioneer* in Allahabad in the North-West Provinces
1888	23	Writing for the *Week's News*, sponsored by the *Pioneer*
1888–9	23–4	*Plain Tales from the Hills; Soldiers Three; The Story of the Gadsbys; In Black and White; The Phantom Rickshaw; Wee Willie Winkie* (Indian Railway Library)
1889	24	Leaves India; travels to America via Rangoon, Singapore, Hong Kong, Japan; crosses America and arrives at Liverpool in October; meets Wolcott Balestier, American publisher and literary agent, who becomes a close friend
1890	25	Literary success in Britain, but suffers breakdown; *Soldiers Three* and other Indian stories published in Britain
1891	26	Visits South Africa, Australia, New Zealand, and India; returns to England; on learning of the death of Wolcott Balestier; *The Light that Failed; Life's Handicap*
1892	27	Marries Caroline (Carrie) Starr Balestier; the bride is given away by Henry James; builds home, 'Naulahka' on

Year	Literary Context	Historical Events
1884		Third Reform Bill in Great Britain
1885	Ezra Pound born	
1886	Stevenson, *Dr Jekyll and Mr Hyde, Kidnapped*	1st Irish Home Rule Bill introduced by Gladstone
1887	Hardy, *The Woodlanders* Haggard, *She*	Queen Victoria's Golden Jubilee
1888	Arnold, *Essays in Criticism* T. S. Eliot born	Whitechapel murders in London
1889	Ibsen's *A Doll's House* first produced in London Stevenson, *The Master of Ballantrae* Baring-Gould collections of Devonshire songs stimulates revival of interest in English folklore	Eiffel Tower built
1890	Booth, *In Darkest England* 2 volumes of Frazer's *The Golden Bough* (12 vols 1911–15) Stanley, *In Darkest Africa*	Cecil Rhodes becomes premier of Cape Colony
1891	Gissing, *New Grub Street* Hardy, *Tess of the D'Urbervilles* Morris, *News from Nowhere*	
1892	Shaw, *Mrs Warren's Profession* Death of Tennyson	

Year	Age	Life
		Balestier family estate in Brattleboro, Vermont; daughter Josephine born in December; *The Naulahka* (written in collaboration with Wolcott Balestier); *Barrack-Room Ballads*
1893	28	*Many Inventions*
1894	29	*The Jungle Book*
1895	30	*The Second Jungle Book*
1896	31	Second daughter Elsie born in February; quarrel with brother-in-law and subsequent lawsuit ends period in Brattleboro; Kiplings move to England; living in Torquay for a time; *The Seven Seas*
1897	32	Son John born in August; family moves to Rottingdean in Sussex; *Captains Courageous*
1898	33	Visits South Africa and Cape Town in particular; meets Cecil Rhodes who becomes a close friend; visits Rhodesia; *The Day's Work*
1899	34	Dangerously ill in New York; Kipling and Elsie recover but Josephine dies of whooping cough; *Stalky and Co.*; *From Sea to Sea*
1900	35	Helps edit army newspaper *The Friend* in South Africa during Boer War

Year	Literary Context	Historical Events
1093	Gissing, *The Odd Women*	Gladstone's 2nd Irish Home Rule Bill rejected by House of Lords
1894	Grossmith, *The Diary of a Nobody* Launch of the *Yellow Book*	Gladstone resigns
1895	Conrad, *Almayer's Folly* Hardy, *Jude the Obscure*	Lumiere brothers show first projected films to a paying audience in Paris
1896	Housman, *A Shropshire Lad* Morris, Kelmscott *Chaucer*	Jameson capitulates to Boers; Rhodes resigns premiership of Cape Colony; Harmsworth and Jones launch *Daily Mail*
1897	Stoker, *Dracula* Wells, *The Invisible Man*	Queen Victoria's Diamond Jubilee; Colonial Conference in London; Marconi founds Wireless Telegraph Company
1898	Wells, *The War of the Worlds*	Death of Gladstone; Kitchener triumphant at Battle of Omdurman in the Sudan; US gain control of Cuba and Philippines after war with Spain; discovery of Radium
1899	Robert Buchanan, 'The Voice of the Hooligan' attacks Kipling's reputation Ellis, *Studies in the Psychology of Sex* Yeats, *Poems*	Boer War – British defeats during 'Black Week' in December at Stormberg, Magersfontein and Colenso; Lord Roberts appointed Commander in Chief, Kitchener his Chief of Staff
1900	Conrad, *Lord Jim* Freud, *The Interpretation of Dreams* Death of Ruskin Death of Wilde	Relief of Mafeking; British Labour Party founded

Year	Age	Life
1901	36	*Kim*
1902	37	Buys 'Batemans' and settles there at Burwash in Sussex; *Just So Stories*
1903	38	*The Five Nations*
1904	39	*Traffics and Discoveries*
1906	41	*Puck of Pook's Hill*
1907	42	Awarded Nobel Prize for Literature; visits Canada; *Collected Verse*
1909	44	*Actions and Reactions; Abaft the Funnel* (in America; not published in Britain until the Sussex Edition in 1938)

Year	Literary Context	Historical Events
1901	Hardy, *Poems of Past and Present*	Death of Queen Victoria; accession of Edward VII; first transatlantic wireless communication
1902	Conan Doyle, *The Hound of the Baskervilles* Conrad, *Heart of Darkness* Wells, *First Men in the Moon*	Colonial Conference in London; death of Rhodes; Boer War ends
1903	Butler, *The Way of All Flesh* Shaw, *Man and Superman*	Women's Social and Political Union formed in Manchester; first aeroplane flight
1904	Conrad, *Nostromo* Barrie, *Peter Pan*	
1906	Baden-Powell, *Scouting for Boys* John Betjeman born	Launch of *Dreadnaught* introduces British naval improvement programme; Liberal government elected in Great Britain; self-government granted to Transvaal
1907	W. H. Auden born Conrad, *The Secret Agent*	Fifth Colonial Conference: self-governing 'colonies' become 'dominions'
1908	Forster, *A Room with a View* Hardy, *The Dynasts*	Women's Freedom League formed; introduction of Old Age Pensions
1909	Death of Swinburne	Alarm over German naval power stimulates growth of Great Britain's Dreadnaught fleet; Indian Council's Act initiates ideas of a self-governing India; Peary reaches North Pole

Year	Age	Life
1910	45	Death of Alice Kipling; *Rewards and Fairies*
1911	46	Death of his father John Lockwood Kipling; *A History of England* (in collaboration with C.R.L. Fletcher)
1913	48	Visits Egypt; *Songs from Books*
1914–18	49–53	Visits to the Front and to the Navy; *The New Army in Training, France at War, The Fringes at the Fleet, Sea Warfare, The Eyes of Asia* and other war pamphlets published
1915	50	Son John reported missing on his first day in action with the Irish Guards at Battle of Loos
1917	52	Becomes member of Imperial War Graves Commission and Trustee for Cecil Rhodes Scholarship Fund; *A Diversity of Creatures*
1918	53	*Twenty Poems*
1919	54	*The Years Between; Rudyard Kipling's Verse: Inclusive Edition* (in three volumes)
1920	55	Visits French battlefields; *Letters of Travel*

Year	Literary Context	Historical Events
1910	Forster, *Howards End* Yeats, *The Green Helmet*	Death of Edward VII and accession of George V; first Post-Impressionist exhibition in London
1911	Conrad, *Under Western Eyes* Masefield, *The Everlasting Mercy*	Amundsen reaches South Pole, followed by Scott's party who perish on the way back
1913	De la Mare, *Peacock Pie* Lawrence, *Sons and Lovers* Mann, *Death in Venice*	Lords reject 3rd Irish Home Rule bill; 'Cat and Mouse' Act
1914	Joyce, *Dubliners* Forster, *Maurice* (not published until 1970) Yeats, *Responsibilities*	Britain declares war on Germany, 4 August, 1914
1915	Ford, *The Good Soldier* Lawrence, *The Rainbow* Woolf, *The Voyage Out*	Einstein's General Theory of Relativity; sinking of *Lusitania*; unprecedented success of D. W. Griffiths film, *Birth of a Nation* in US
1917	Burroughs, *Tarzan of The Apes* Eliot, *Prufrock and Other Observations*	Russian Revolution
1918	Brooke, *Collected Poems* Hopkins, *Poems* Strachey, *Eminent Victorians* Death of Wilfred Owen	Great War ends; Representation of the People Act grants voting rights to women aged 30 and over
1919	Eliot, 'Tradition and the Individual Talent' Hardy, *Collected Poems*	Treaty of Versailles
1920	Shaw, *Heartbreak House*	League of Nations formed; Great Britain wartime conscription ends
1921	Lawrence, *Women in Love*	Irish Free State established
1922	Eliot, *The Waste Land* Joyce, *Ulysses*	Regular radio broadcasting begins in Britain

Year	Age	Life
1923	58	*The Irish Guards in the Great War* (2 vols); *Land and Sea Tales for Scouts and Guides*
1924	59	Daughter Elsie marries Captain George Bambridge; *Songs for Youth*
1926	61	*Debits and Credits*
1927	62	Visits Brazil
1928	63	*A Book of Words* (collected speeches)
1929	64	Visits war graves in Egypt and Palestine
1930	65	Visits West Indies; *Thy Servant a Dog*
1932	67	*Limits and Renewals*
1933	68	*Souvenirs of France*
1934	69	*Collected Dog Stories*
1936	71	18 January, Rudyard Kipling dies at Middlesex Hospital, London

Year	Literary Context	Historical Events
1923	Yeats awarded Nobel Prize	
1924	Forster, *A Passage to India* Wren, *Beau Geste* Death of Conrad	First Labour government in Britain, under MacDonald
1926	T. E. Lawrence, *Seven Pillars of Wisdom* Milne, *Winnie-the-Pooh*	General Strike in Britain
1927	Woolf, *To the Lighthouse* Kipling Society founded.	Lindbergh makes first solo transatlantic flight
1928	Hall, *The Well of Loneliness* Lawrence, *Lady Chatterley's Lover; Collected Poems* Woolf, *Orlando* Yeats, *The Tower* Death of Hardy	Women's Suffrage Bill passed in Britain
1929	Graves, *Goodbye to all That* Hemingway, *A Farewell To Arms* Remarque, *All Quiet on the Western Front* Woolf, *A Room of One's Own*	Wall Street Crash
1930	Auden, *Poems* Empson, *Seven Types of Ambiguity* Death of D. H. Lawrence	Gandhi opens civil disobedience campaign in India
1932	Lawrence, *Last Poems* Leavis, *New Bearings in English Poetry*	
1933	Wells, *The Shape of Things to Come*	Hitler comes to power in Germany
1934	Priestley, *An English Journey*	
1936		Death of George V; accession of Edward VIII

Introduction

In an essay calling for a reappraisal of Rudyard Kipling's poetry, T. S. Eliot addressed some of the political problems which rise from his work. For Kipling, he stated, 'the Empire was not merely an idea, a good idea or a bad one; it was something of the reality of which he felt.' Eliot was writing in 1941, during a time of war and five years after Kipling's death. Given the charges of aggressiveness and militarism levelled at Kipling's work during his lifetime, Eliot's advocacy was timely, and foremost among others to signal a renewed interest in his work in that decade.

Literary reputations respond to the values of different times and circumstances; Kipling's reputation offers an outstanding example. His lifetime, from 1865 to 1936, spans not only that central period of Empire with which Victorian Britain was so obsessed, but also encompasses its decline and disfavour. His reputation as a poet – even *the* poet – of Empire often remains as a charge against him, even as his work has remained very popular. From 1899 onwards, when the critic Robert Buchanan attacked him as a poet of 'false' rather than 'true' imperialism, evaluations of Kipling's work have had to take account of its political implications, with varying degrees of distaste. Buchanan was incensed at the 'brutality' of Kipling's characters, and at the warmongering and blasphemy he felt they incited. Such writing, he declared, went against the truly civilizing ideals of the British Empire. As well as setting in train a critical reaction to Kipling's work which it has never entirely lost, his review also indicates how contradictory in themselves ideas of Empire could be. It shows too how closely linked they were with prevailing liberal notions of literature and culture. It is perhaps not surprising that, in spite of widespread acclaim in the 1880s and 1890s, by the time of Kipling's death in the much-changed political circumstances of the inter-war years his critical reputation was particularly low.

Yet as Buchanan's review implies, Kipling was decidedly opposi-tional in his writing. This occurs as much in literary as in political alignment, and the two are not always wholly divisible. The titles of his earliest collections, *Departmental Ditties* (1886) and *Barrack-Room Ballads and other Verses* (1892), emphasize their distance from the prevailing *fin-de-siècle* aestheticism as much as they reflect the concerns of the civil and military services of Anglo-India. By proclaiming their engagement with the realities of modern life, they also stand against an avant-garde perceived as languidly introspective.

Discussion of the comparative 'femininities' of poets such as Tennyson and Swinburne in the mid-Victorian period contributed in the 1890s to a wider debate in which anxieties about the effeminization of literature and art were expressed in nationalist, even racist, overtones. In Kipling's early poem 'In Partibus', aesthetes are not men but 'things' aligned with women and animals in their 'artistic' discussions:

> But I consort with long-haired things
> In velvet collar-rolls,
> Who talk about the Aims of Art
> And 'theories' and 'goals,'
> And moo and coo with women-folk
> About their blessed souls.

Similarly, in 'The *Mary Gloster*' the dying Sir Anthony reproaches his aesthete son, 'For you muddled with books and pictures, an' china an' etchin's an' fans,/ And your rooms at college was beastly – more like a whore's than a man's . . .' His querulous voice, and our awareness of his silent son, might warn us against accepting Sir Anthony's judgements at face value. However, with the introduction of images of decadence and decline ('There isn't even a grandchild, and the Gloster family's done . . .'), theme and style combine to give an ironic gloss on the status of art.

Kipling emphasizes the 'masculine' clarity of narrative rather than reflective verse, in opposition to what Max Nordau, a contemporary commentator, summed up as 'the aesthetics of the Dusk of Nations' where 'forms lose their outlines, and are dissolved in floating mist'. References to literary forms in the titles of Kipling's verse often possess a secondary national or cultural identity. 'Puck's Song' proclaims its 'Englishness' through the allusion to Shakespeare, 'The Ballad of East and West' and 'A St Helena Lullaby' operate through overlapping geographical and historical locations, as does (note the pun) 'The White Man's Burden'. In these cases, the light, popular form, whether song, ballad, lullaby or burden, renders its subject-matter comfortingly immediate. Conversely, the formal artifice of 'Sestina of the *Tramp-Royal*' elevates a character which a more conventional writer might have treated as humble or comic.

Ditties and ballads belong to a narrative world which is essentially communal; they demand to be spoken rather than read in isolation. In these poems mnemonic devices abound; particularly in 'The Ballad of East and West' where repetitions of the heavily accented lines and Kipling's use of the past continuous tense, recall the oral patterning found in folk ballads and biblical narratives. Easily dismissed as the stuff of music-hall monologue or schoolboy recitation, the poem also appeals to a popular audience through its codes of romance and melodrama.

Kipling's use of such codes emphasizes notions of male honour which cut across racial and class differences. With Kamal and the Colonel's son in 'The Ballad of East and West', where 'never the twain shall meet' until 'two strong men stand face to face', it is action, not reflection, which promotes the bond between men and imaginatively creates union. However, poems like 'Gunga Din' and 'Fuzzy-Wuzzy' indicate how utopian these premises are, for in each case the British soldier-speaker's admiration for the Hindu water-carrier and Sudanese warrior is expressed in language which underplays their specific racial and cultural distinctiveness: 'for all 'is dirty 'ide / 'E was white, clear white, inside', aligns white and black skin colour with cleanliness and dirt, health and disease, while 'Fuzzy-Wuzzy', the 'first-class fighting man', is described in both childlike and animal terms. Both poems celebrate their protagonists in terms of an evolutionary continuum where the white man is uppermost.

Perhaps the best-known and most popular of Kipling's poems is 'If—'. Its own prescriptives for masculinity are generally taken at face value. Yet 'If—' also has a heavily ironic side to it, with the repeated conditionals ('If . . .', 'Or . . .', 'And yet . . .') indicating that behind this ideal lies a harsh and brutal world where manliness is as much down to luck and the need for a psychological armoury as it is to abstract codes. A major part of that armoury, essential to the success of the British Empire, was Standard English, the language of government, the ruling classes and the civil service.

Knowledge of English literature was a mandatory requirement for all candidates for the Indian Civil Service from 1855.

Kipling's barrack-room verse in particular challenged the critical establishment at a crucial period in its imperialist history. His use of regional accent, dialect, and the demotic, signified at one level the powerlessness as well as crudeness of the lower classes on which the services drew for their lower ranks. Yet however brutal it might seem, it also affirmed the endurance of British fighting men precisely in terms of their *emotionality*, where regional identities overlay their voices with related values of warmth, vigour and communality. The tone of Robert Buchanan's article made it clear that this ran counter to dominant ideals of imperialist masculinity, where self-control was expressed in language: 'It seems ... a favourite condition with Mr Kipling, when he celebrates acts of manly daring, that his subjects should be mad drunk, and, at any rate, as drunken in their language as possible'. Although Kipling's poems have often been said to speak for the underdog, defined in terms of class and race (though not, significantly, for women), it is in their challenge to ideals of masculinity that they are subversive.

Fears of emotional excess and of the power of the female also run through Kipling's verse. Most typically they are to be found in variations on that archetype of decadence, the 'fatal woman'. Whether it is Sir Anthony's ship/wife in 'The *Mary Gloster*', to which/whom he intends to be lashed as he goes to his death beneath the waves; or 'The Female of the Species' who, 'deadlier than the male', must be kept from Council and Government; or 'The Vampire', the modern woman who metaphorically drains her partner of his money, honour and faith by her demands ('Seeing at last, she could never know why/ And never could understand!'); representations of the *femme fatale* link anxieties of power with fears of female insatiability.

Since Eliot's essay of 1941, the redefinition of literature within a broader cultural framework has revealed a more multi-faceted Kipling. If, for later readers imperialist 'Law', as conventionally understood in his verse, is a system of authority which has failed more people than it has benefited, then it is worth looking for those elements in Kipling's work which also go 'against the grain' of such a reading. For it is here that we may also see imperialist myth-making exposed and opened up for scrutiny.

'The Way through the Woods', for example, offers a version of an

'England' planted and coppiced, which is invested in the central figure of a keeper who 'sees' a past which lies beneath the surface landscape. It recalls cyclical versions of history found in 'Recessional', where warnings that 'all our pomp of yesterday / Is one with Nineveh and Tyre!' imply the inevitable fall of Empires. In 'Puck's Song', marks on the landscape are traces, mysteries, which keep the past imaginatively present. Such a reading of 'The Way through the Woods' offers an idyll of England which might both justify the continuation of imperialist endeavours to its admirers and serve as an escape or refuge from their anxieties. Either way the vision is regenerative; it is not difficult to see the poem's appeal when it first appeared in *Rewards and Fairies* in 1910.

However, as the breakdown of the British Empire became increasingly apparent in the early years of the twentieth century, such a poem, poised between ideas of imperialist progress and decline, can be read quite differently. It can be given a different emphasis, where the ghostly female rider represents forces of difference – of race, class and gender. It is not only the keeper 'seeing', but you, the reader, *hearing* the hooves beating and the skirt swishing which establishes their ghostly presence as part of this scene. This much-loved England of 'misty solitudes' is not what it seems. With its blurred edges, its planted trees which block a road both done and 'undone', human endeavour would seem to be turning back on itself. Read in this way, any picture of 'England' we get is one in which the validity of its 'true' character is open to question and even perhaps to change.

So, too, with other poems in this collection, whose unexpected ambiguities challenge Kipling's reputation as the mouthpiece of a reactionary establishment. Rather, we should see in his work a rich and multiple vocality whose own internal contradictions expose the tensions contained in ideas of art and Empire alike.

JAN HEWITT

Rudyard Kipling

The Post That Fitted

Though tangled and twisted the course of true love,
This ditty explains,
No tangle's so tangled it cannot improve
If the Lover has brains.

Ere the steamer bore him Eastward, Sleary was engaged to marry
An attractive girl at Tunbridge, whom he called 'my little Carrie.'
Sleary's pay was very modest; Sleary was the other way.
Who can cook a two-plate dinner on eight poor rupees a day?

Long he pondered o'er the question in his scantly furnished
    quarters— 5
Then proposed to Minnie Boffkin, eldest of Judge Boffkin's
    daughters.
Certainly an impecunious Subaltern was not a catch,
But the Boffkins knew that Minnie mightn't make another
    match.

So they recognised the business and, to feed and clothe the bride,
Got him made a Something Something somewhere on the
    Bombay side. 10
Anyhow, the billet carried pay enough for him to marry—
As the artless Sleary put it:—'Just the thing for me and Carrie.'

Did he, therefore, jilt Miss Boffkin—impulse of a baser mind?
No! He started epileptic fits of an appalling kind.
[Of his *modus operandi* only this much I could gather:— 15
'Pears's shaving sticks will give you little taste and lots of lather.']

Frequently in public places his affliction used to smite
Sleary with distressing vigour—always in the Boffkins' sight.
Ere a week was over Minnie weepingly returned his ring,
Told him his 'unhappy weakness' stopped all thought of
    marrying. 20

Sleary bore the information with a chastened holy joy,—
Epileptic fits don't matter in Political employ,—

Wired three short words to Carrie—took his ticket, packed his
    kit—
Bade farewell to Minnie Boffkin in one last, long, lingering fit.

Four weeks later, Carrie Sleary read—and laughed until she
    wept—   25
Mrs Boffkin's warning letter on the 'wretched epilept.' . . .
Year by year, in pious patience, vengeful Mrs Boffkin sits
Waiting for the Sleary babies to develop Sleary's fits.

Sestina of the Tramp-Royal

Speakin' in general, I 'ave tried 'em all—
The 'appy roads that take you o'er the world.
Speakin' in general, I 'ave found them good
For such as cannot use one bed too long,
But must get 'ence, the same as I 'ave done,   5
An' go observin' matters till they die.

What do it matter where or 'ow we die,
So long as we've our 'ealth to watch it all—
The different ways that different things are done,
An' men an' women lovin' in this world;   10
Takin' our chances as they come along,
An' when they ain't, pretendin' they are good?

In cash or credit—no, it aren't no good;
You 'ave to 'ave the 'abit or you'd die,
Unless you lived your life but one day long,   15
Nor didn't prophesy nor fret at all,
But drew your tucker some'ow from the world,
An' never bothered what you might ha' done.

But, Gawd, what things are they I 'aven't done?
I've turned my 'and to most, an' turned it good,   20
In various situations round the world—

For 'im that doth not work must surely die;
But that's no reason man should labour all
'Is life on one same shift—life's none so long.

Therefore, from job to job I've moved along.   25
Pay couldn't 'old me when my time was done,
For something in my 'ead upset it all,
Till I 'ad dropped whatever 'twas for good,
An', out at sea, be'eld the dock-lights die,
An' met my mate—the wind that tramps the world!   30

It's like a book, I think, this bloomin' world,
Which you can read and care for just so long,
But presently you feel that you will die
Unless you get the page you're readin' done,
An' turn another—likely not so good;   35
But what you're after is to turn 'em all.

Gawd bless this world! Whatever she 'ath done—
Excep' when awful long—I've found it good.
So write, before I die, "E liked it all!'

The Explorer

'There's no sense in going further—it's the edge of cultivation,'
So they said, and I believed it—broke my land and sowed my
    crop—
Built my barns and strung my fences in the little border station
    Tucked away below the foothills where the trails run out and
    stop:

Till a voice, as bad as Conscience, rang interminable changes   5
    On one everlasting Whisper day and night repeated—so:
'Something hidden. Go and find it. Go and look behind the
    Ranges—

'Something lost behind the Ranges. Lost and waiting for you.
    Go!'

So I went, worn out of patience; never told my nearest
    neighbours—
    Stole away with pack and ponies—left 'em drinking in the
        town;   10
And the faith that moveth mountains didn't seem to help my
    labours
    As I faced the sheer main-ranges, whipping up and leading
        down.

March by march I puzzled through 'em, turning flanks and
    dodging shoulders,
    Hurried on in hope of water, headed back for lack of grass;
Till I camped above the tree-line—drifted snow and naked
    boulders—   15
    Felt free air astir to windward—knew I'd stumbled on the Pass.

'Thought to name it for the finder: but that night the Norther
    found me—
    Froze and killed the plains-bred ponies; so I called the camp
        Despair
(It's the Railway Gap today, though). Then my Whisper waked to
    hound me:—
    'Something lost behind the Ranges. Over yonder! Go you
        there!'   20

Then I knew, the while I doubted—knew His Hand was certain
    o'er me.
    Still—it might be self-delusion—scores of better men had
        died—
I could reach the township living, but . . . He knows what terror
    tore me . . .
    But I didn't . . . but I didn't. I went down the other side,

Till the snow ran out in flowers, and the flowers turned to aloes,
    And the aloes sprung to thickets and a brimming stream ran
        by;
But the thickets dwined to thorn-scrub, and the water drained
    to shallows,

And I dropped again on desert—blasted earth, and blasting
    sky. . . .

I remember lighting fires; I remember sitting by 'em;
    I remember seeing faces, hearing voices, through the smoke; 30
I remember they were fancy—for I threw a stone to try 'em.
    'Something lost behind the Ranges' was the only word they
        spoke.

I remember going crazy. I remember that I knew it
    When I heard myself hallooing to the funny folk I saw.
Very full of dreams that desert, but my two legs took me through
    it . . .   35
    And I used to watch 'em moving with the toes all black and
        raw.

But at last the country altered—White Man's country past
        disputing—
    Rolling grass and open timber, with a hint of hills behind—
There I found me food and water, and I lay a week recruiting.
    Got my strength and lost my nightmares. Then I entered on
        my find.   40

Thence I ran my first rough survey—chose my trees and blazed
        and ringed 'em—
    Week by week I pried and sampled—week by week my findings
        grew.
Saul he went to look for donkeys, and by God he found a
        kingdom!
    But by God, who sent His Whisper, I had struck the worth of
        two!

Up along the hostile mountains, where the hair-poised snow-slide
        shivers—   45
    Down and through the big fat marshes that the virgin ore-bed
        stains,
Till I heard the mile-wide mutterings of unimagined rivers,
    And beyond the nameless timber saw illimitable plains!

Plotted sites of future cities, traced the easy grades between 'em;

Watched unharnessed rapids wasting fifty thousand head an
    hour;   50
Counted leagues of water-frontage through the axe-ripe woods
    that screen 'em—
Saw the plant to feed a people—up and waiting for the power!

Well I know who'll take the credit—all the clever chaps that
    followed—
Came, a dozen men together—never knew my desert-fears;
Tracked me by the camps I'd quitted, used the water-holes I'd
    hollowed.   55
    They'll go back and do the talking. *They'll* be called the
    Pioneers!

They will find my sites of townships—not the cities that I set
    there.
They will rediscover rivers—not my rivers heard at night.
By my own old marks and bearings they will show me how to get
    there,
    By the lonely cairns I builded they will guide my feet aright.   60

Have I named one single river? Have I claimed one single acre?
    Have I kept one single nugget—(barring samples)? No, not I!
Because my price was paid me ten times over by my Maker.
    But you wouldn't understand it. You go up and occupy.

Ores you'll find there; wood and cattle; water-transit sure and
    steady   65
    (That should keep the railway-rates down), coal and iron at
    your doors.
God took care to hide that country till He judged His people
    ready,
    Then He chose me for His Whisper, and I've found it, and it's
    yours!

Yes, your 'Never-never country'—yes, your 'edge of cultivation'
    And 'no sense in going further'—till I crossed the range to
    see.   70
God forgive me! No, *I* didn't. It's God's present to our nation.
    Anybody might have found it, but—His Whisper came to Me!

McAndrew's Hymn

Lord, Thou hast made this world below the shadow of a dream,
An', taught by time, I tak' it so—exceptin' always Steam.
From coupler-flange to spindle-guide I see Thy Hand, O God—
Predestination in the stride o' yon connectin'-rod.
John Calvin might ha' forged the same—enorrmous, certain,
    slow— 5
Ay, wrought it in the furnace-flame—*my* 'Institutio.'
I cannot get my sleep tonight; old bones are hard to please;
I'll stand the middle watch up here—alone wi' God an' these
My engines, after ninety days o' race an' rack an' strain
Through all the seas of all Thy world, slam-bangin' home again.
Slam-bang too much—they knock a wee—the crosshead-gibs are
    loose,
But thirty thousand mile o' sea has gied them fair excuse. . . .
Fine, clear an' dark—a full-draught breeze, wi' Ushant out o'
    sight,
An' Ferguson relievin' Hay. Old girl, ye'll walk to-night!
His wife's at Plymouth. . . . Seventy—One—Two—Three since he
    began— 15
Three turns for Mistress Ferguson . . . and who's to blame the
    man?
There's none at any port for me, by drivin' fast or slow,
Since Elsie Campbell went to Thee, Lord, thirty years ago.
(The year the *Sarah Sands* was burned. Oh, roads we used to
    tread,
Fra' Maryhill to Pollokshaws—fra' Govan to Parkhead!) 20
Not but they're ceevil on the Board. Ye'll hear Sir Kenneth say:
'Good morrn, McAndrew! Back again? An' how's your bilge
    to-day?'
Miscallin' technicalities but handin' me my chair
To drink Madeira wi' three Earls—the auld Fleet Engineer
That started as a boiler-whelp—when steam and he were low. 25
I mind the time we used to serve a broken pipe wi' tow!
Ten pound was all the pressure then—Eh! Eh!—a man wad
    drive;
An' here, our workin' gauges give one hunder sixty-five!

We're creepin' on wi' each new rig—less weight an' larger
  power;
There'll be the loco-boiler next an' thirty mile an hour!   30
Thirty an' more. What I ha' seen since ocean-steam began
Leaves me na doot for the machine: but what about the man?
The man that counts, wi' all his runs, one million mile o' sea:
Four time the span from earth to moon. . . . How far, O Lord,
  from Thee
That wast beside him night an' day? Ye mind my first typhoon? 35
It scoughed the skipper on his way to jock wi' the saloon.
Three feet were on the stokehold-floor—just slappin' to an' fro—
An' cast me on a furnace-door. I have the marks to show.
Marks! I ha' marks o' more than burns—deep in my soul an'
  black,
An' times like this, when things go smooth, my wickudness
  comes back.   40
The sins o' four an' forty years, all up an' down the seas,
Clack an' repeat like valves half-fed. . . . Forgie's our trespasses!
Nights when I'd come on deck to mark, wi' envy in my gaze,
The couples kittlin' in the dark between the funnel-stays;
Years when I raked the Ports wi' pride to fill my cup o' wrong—45
Judge not, O Lord, my steps aside at Gay Street in Hong Kong!
Blot out the wastrel hours of mine in sin when I abode—
Jane Harrigan's an' Number Nine, The Reddick an' Grant Road!
An' waur than all—my crownin' sin—rank blasphemy an' wild.
I was not four and twenty then—Ye wadna judge a child?   50
I'd seen the Tropics first that run—new fruit, new smells, new
  air—
How could I tell—blind-fou wi' sun—the Deil was lurkin' there?
By day like playhouse-scenes the shore slid past our sleepy eyes;
By night those soft, lasceevious stars leered from those velvet
  skies,
In port (we used no cargo-steam) I'd daunder down the streets—55
An ijjit grinnin' in a dream—for shells an' parrakeets,
An' walkin'-sticks o' carved bamboo an' blowfish stuffed an'
  dried—
Fillin' my bunk wi' rubbishry the Chief put overside.
Till, off Sambawa Head, Ye mind, I heard a land-breeze ca',
Milk-warm wi' breath o' spice an' bloom: 'McAndrew, come
  awa'!'   60

Firm, clear an' low—no haste, no hate—the ghostly whisper
  went,
Just statin' eevidential facts beyon' all argument:
'Your mither's God's a graspin' deil, the shadow o' yoursel',
'Got out o' books by meenisters clean daft on Heaven an' Hell.
'They mak' him in the Broomielaw, o' Glasgie cold an' dirt, 65
'A jealous, pridefu' fetich, lad, that's only strong to hurt
'Ye'll not go back to Him again an' kiss His red-hot rod,
'But come wi' Us' (Now, who were *They?*) 'an' know the Leevin'
  God,
'That does not kipper souls for sport or break a life in jest,
'But swells the ripenin' cocoanuts an' ripes the woman's breast.'
An' there it stopped—cut off—no more—that quiet, certain
  voice—
For me, six months o' twenty-four, to leave or take at choice.
'Twas on me like a thunderclap—it racked me through an'
  through—
Temptation past the show o' speech, unnameable an' new—
The Sin against the Holy Ghost? . . . An' under all, our screw. 75

That storm blew by but left behind her anchor-shiftin' swell.
Thou knowest all my heart an' mind, Thou knowest, Lord, I
  fell—
Third on the *Mary Gloster* then, and first that night in Hell!
Yet was Thy Hand beneath my head, about my feet Thy Care—
Fra' Deli clear to Torres Strait, the trial o' despair, 80
But when we touched the Barrier Reef Thy answer to my
  prayer! . . .
We dared na run that sea by night but lay an' held our fire,
An' I was drowsin' on the hatch—sick—sick wi' doubt an' tire:
'Better the sight of eyes that see than wanderin' o' desire!'
Ye mind that word? Clear as our gongs—again, an' once again, 86
When rippin' down through coral-trash ran out our moorin'-
  chain:
An', by Thy Grace, I had the Light to see my duty plain.
Light on the engine-room—no more—bright as our carbons
  burn.
I've lost it since a thousand times, but never past return!

*

Obsairve! Per annum we'll have here two thousand souls
        aboard—   90
Think not I dare to justify myself before the Lord,
But—average fifteen hunder souls safe-borne fra' port to port—
I *am* o' service to my kind.   Ye wadna blame the thought?
Maybe they steam from Grace to Wrath—to sin by folly led—
It isna mine to judge their path—their lives are on my head.   95
Mine at the last—when all is done it all comes back to me,
The fault that leaves six thousand ton a log upon the sea.
We'll tak' one stretch—three weeks an' odd by ony road ye
        steer—
Fra' Cape Town east to Wellington—ye need an engineer.
Fail there—ye've time to weld your shaft—ay, eat it, ere ye're
        spoke;   100
Or make Kerguelen under sail—three jiggers burned wi' smoke!
An' home again—the Rio run: it's no child's play to go
Steamin' to bell for fourteen days o' snow an' floe an' blow.
The bergs like kelpies overside that girn an' turn an' shift
Whaur, grindin' like the Mills o' God, goes by the big South
        drift.   105
(Hail, Snow and Ice that praise the Lord.   I've met them at their
        work,
An' wished we had anither route or they anither kirk.)
Yon's strain, hard strain, o' head an' hand, for though Thy
        Power brings
All skill to naught, Ye'll understand a man must think o' things.
Then, at the last, we'll get to port an' hoist their baggage
        clear—   110
The passengers, wi' gloves an' canes—an' this is what I'll hear:
'Well, thank ye for a pleasant voyage.   The tender's comin'
        now.'
While I go testin' follower-bolts an' watch the skipper bow.
They've words for every one but me—shake hands wi' half the
        crew,
Except the dour Scots engineer, the man they never knew.   115
An' yet I like the wark for all we've dam'-few pickin's here—
No pension, an' the most we'll earn's four hunder pound a year.

Better myself abroad?   Maybe.   *I'd* sooner starve than sail
Wi' such as call a snifter-rod *ross*. . . . French for nightingale.
Commeesion on my stores?   Some do; but I cannot afford   120
To lie like stewards wi' patty-pans.   I'm older than the Board.
A bonus on the coal I save?   Ou ay, the Scots are close,
But when I grudge the strength Ye gave I'll grudge their food to
    those.
(There's bricks that I might recommend—an' clink the fire-bars
    cruel.
No! Welsh—Wangarti at the worst—an' damn all patent fuel!) 125
Inventions? Ye must stay in port to mak' a patent pay.
My Deeferential Valve-Gear taught me how that business lay.
I blame no chaps wi' clearer heads for aught they make or sell.
I found that I could not invent an' look to these as well.
So, wrestled wi' Apollyon—Nah!—fretted like a bairn—   130
But burned the workin'-plans last run, wi' all I hoped to earn.
Ye know how hard an Idol dies, an' what that meant to me—
E'en tak' it for a sacrifice acceptable to Thee. . . .
Below there! Oiler! What's your wark? Ye find it runnin' hard?
Ye needn't swill the cup wi' oil—this isn't the Cunard!   135
Ye thought? Ye are not paid to think. Go, sweat that off again!
Tck! Tck!   It's deeficult to sweer nor tak' The Name in vain!
Men, ay, an women, call me stern.   Wi' these to oversee,
Ye'll note I've little time to burn on social repartee.
The bairns see what their elders miss; they'll hunt me to an'
    fro,   140
Till for the sake of—well, a kiss—I tak' 'em down below.
That minds me of our Viscount loon—Sir Kenneth's kin—the
    chap
Wi' Russia-leather tennis-shoon an' spar-decked yachtin'-cap.
I showed him round last week, o'er all—an' at the last says he:
'Mister McAndrew, don't you think steam spoils romance at
    sea?'   145
Damned ijjit! I'd been doon that morn to see what ailed the
    throws,
Manholin', on my back—the cranks three inches off my nose.
Romance! Those first-class passengers they like it very well,
Printed an' bound in little books; but why don't poets tell?

I'm sick of all their quirks an' turns—the loves an' doves they
    dream—   150
Lord, send a man like Robbie Burns to sing the Song o' Steam!
To match wi' Scotia's noblest speech yon orchestra sublime
Whaurto—uplifted like the Just—the tail rods mark the time.
The crank-throws give the double-bass, the feed-pump sobs an'
    heaves,
An' now the main eccentrics start their quarrel on the sheaves:
Her time, her own appointed time, the rocking link-head bides,
Till—hear that note?—the rod's return whings glimmerin'
    through the guides.
They're all awa'! True beat, full power, the clangin' chorus goes
Clear to the tunnel where they sit, my purrin' dynamoes.
Interdependence absolute, foreseen, ordained, decreed,   160
To work, Ye'll note, at ony tilt an' every rate o' speed.
Fra' skylight-lift to furnace-bars, backed, bolted, braced an'
    stayed,
An' singin' like the Mornin' Stars for joy that they are made;
While, out o' touch o' vanity, the sweatin' thrust-block says:
'Not unto us the praise, or man—not unto us the praise!'   165
Now, a' together, hear them lift their lesson—theirs an' mine:
'Law, Orrder, Duty an' Restraint, Obedience, Discipline!'
Mill, forge an' try-pit taught them that when roarin' they arose,
An' whiles I wonder if a soul was gied them wi' the blows.
Oh for a man to weld it then, in one trip-hammer strain,   170
Till even first-class passengers could tell the meanin' plain!
But no one cares except mysel' that serve an' understand
My seven thousand horse-power here.   Eh, Lord!   They're
    grand—they're grand!
Uplift am I?   When first in store the new-made beasties stood,
Were Ye cast down that breathed the Word declarin' all things
    good?   175
Not so!   O' that warld-liftin' joy no after-fall could vex,
Ye've left a glimmer still to cheer the Man—the Arrtifex!
That holds, in spite o' knock and scale, o' friction, waste an' slip,
An' by that light—now, mark my word—we'll build the Perfect
    Ship.
I'll never last to judge her lines or take her curve—not I.   180
But I ha' lived an' I ha' worked.   Be thanks to Thee, Most High!
An' I ha' done what I ha' done—judge Thou if ill or well—

Always Thy Grace preventin' me. . . .
                  Losh! Yon's the 'Stand-by' bell.
Pilot so soon?   His flare it is.   The mornin'-watch is set.
Well, God be thanked, as I was sayin', I'm no Pelagian yet.   185
Now I'll tak' on. . . .
    'Morrn, Ferguson. Man, have ye ever thought
What your good leddy costs in coal? , , , I'll burn 'em down to port.

The *Mary Gloster*

I've paid for your sickest fancies; I've humoured your crackedest
    whim—
Dick, it's your daddy, dying; you've got to listen to him!
Good for a fortnight, am I? The doctor told you? He lied.
I shall go under by morning, and—— Put that nurse outside.
'Never seen death yet, Dickie? Well, now is your time to learn,   5
And you'll wish you held my record before it comes to your turn.
Not counting the Line and the Foundry, the Yards and the
    village, too,
I've made myself and a million; but I'm damned if I made you.
Master at two-and-twenty, and married at twenty-three—
Ten thousand men on the pay-roll, and forty freighters at sea!   10
Fifty years between 'em, and every year of it fight,
And now I'm Sir Anthony Gloster, dying, a baronite:
For I lunched with his Royal 'Ighness—what was it the papers
    had?
'Not least of our merchant-princes.' Dickie, that's me, your dad!
I didn't begin with askings. *I* took my job and I stuck;   15
I took the chances they wouldn't, an' now they're calling it luck.
Lord, what boats I've handled—rotten and leaky and old—
Ran 'em, or—opened the bilge-cock, precisely as I was told.
Grub that 'ud bind you crazy, and crews that 'ud turn you grey,
And a big fat lump of insurance to cover the risk on the way.   20
The others they dursn't do it; they said they valued their life
(They've served me since as skippers). *I* went, and I took my wife.
Over the world I drove 'em, married at twenty-three,

And your mother saving the money and making a man of me.
I was content to be master, but she said there was better behind: 25
She took the chances I wouldn't, and I followed your mother
　　　blind.
She egged me to borrow the money, an' she helped me to clear
　　　the loan,
When we bought half-shares in a cheap 'un and hoisted a flag of
　　　our own.
Patching and coaling on credit, and living the Lord knew how,
We started the Red Ox freighters—we've eight-and-thirty now. 30
And those were the days of clippers, and the freights were clipper-
　　　freights,
And we knew we were making our fortune, but she died in
　　．Macassar Straits—
By the Little Paternosters, as you come to the Union Bank
And we dropped her in fourteen fathom: I pricked it off where she
　　　sank.
Owners we were, full owners, and the boat was christened for
　　　her, 35
And she died in the *Mary Gloster*. My heart, how young we were!
So I went on a spree round Java and well-nigh ran her ashore,
But your mother came and warned me and I wouldn't liquor no
　　　more:
Strict I stuck to my business, afraid to stop or I'd think,
Saving the money (she warned me), and letting the other men
　　　drink. 40
And I met M'Cullough in London (I'd saved five 'undred then),
And 'tween us we started the Foundry—three forges and twenty
　　　men.
Cheap repairs for the cheap 'uns. It paid, and the business grew;
For I bought me a steam-lathe patent, and that was a gold mine
　　　too.
'Cheaper to build 'em than buy 'em,' I said, but M'Cullough he
　　　shied, 45
And we wasted a year in talking before we moved to the Clyde.
And the Lines were all beginning, and we all of us started fair,
Building our engines like houses and staying the boilers square.
But M'Cullough 'e wanted cabins with marble and maple and all,
And Brussels an' Utrecht velvet, and baths and a Social Hall, 50
And pipes for closets all over, and cutting the frames too light,

But M'Cullough he died in the Sixties, and—— Well, I'm dying
    to-night. . . .
I knew—*I* knew what was coming, when we bid on the *Byfleet*'s
    keel—
They piddled and piffled with iron. I'd given my orders for steel!
Steel and the first expansions. It paid, I tell you, it paid,   55
When we came with our nine knot freighters and collared the
    long-run trade!
And they asked me how I did it, and I gave 'em the Scripture text,
'You keep your light so shining a little in front o' the next!'
They copied all they could follow, but they couldn't copy my
    mind,
And I left 'em sweating and stealing a year and a half behind.   60
Then came the armour-contracts, but that was M'Cullough's
    side;
He was always best in the Foundry, but better, perhaps, he died.
I went through his private papers; the notes was plainer than
    print;
And I'm no fool to finish if a man'll give me a hint.
(I remember his widow was angry.) So I saw what his drawings
    meant,   65
And I started the six-inch rollers, and it paid me sixty per cent.
Sixty per cent *with* failures, and more than twice we could do,
And a quarter-million to credit, and I saved it all for you!
I thought—it doesn't matter—you seemed to favour your ma,
But you're nearer forty than thirty, and I know the kind you
    are.   70
Harrer an' Trinity College! I ought to ha' sent you to sea—
But I stood you an education, an' what have you done for me?
The things I knew was proper you wouldn't thank me to give,
And the things I knew was rotten you said was the way to live.
For you muddled with books and pictures, an' china an' etchin's
    an' fans,   75
And your rooms at college was beastly—more like a whore's
    than a man's;
Till you married that thin-flanked woman, as white and as stale
    as a bone,
An' she gave you your social nonsense; but where's that kid o'
    your own?
I've seen your carriages blocking the half o' the Cromwell Road,

But never the doctor's brougham to help the missus unload.   80
(So there isn't even a grandchild, an' the Gloster family's done.)
Not like your mother, she isn't. *She* carried her freight each run.
But they died, the pore little beggars! At sea she had 'em—they
    died.
Only you, an' you stood it. You haven't stood much beside.
Weak, a liar, and idle, and mean as a collier's whelp   85
Nosing for scraps in the galley. No help—my son was no help!
So he gets three 'undred thousand, in trust and the interest paid.
I wouldn't give it you, Dickie—you see, I made it in trade.
You're saved from soiling your fingers, and if you have no child,
It all comes back to the business. 'Gad, won't your wife be wild! 90
'Calls and calls in her carriage, her 'andkerchief up to 'er eye:
'Daddy! dear daddy's dyin'!' and doing her best to cry.
Grateful? Oh, yes, I'm grateful, but keep her away from here.
Your mother 'ud never ha' stood 'er, and, anyhow, women are
    queer. . . .
There's women will say I've married a second time. Not quite!   95
But give pore Aggie a hundred, and tell her your lawyers'll fight.
She was the best o' the boiling—you'll meet her before it ends.
I'm in for a row with the mother—I'll leave you settle my friends.
For a man he must go with a woman, which women don't
    understand—
Or the sort that say they can see it they aren't the marrying
    brand.   100
But I wanted to speak o' your mother that's Lady Gloster still;
I'm going to up and see her, without its hurting the will.
Here! Take your hand off the bell-pull. Five thousand's waiting
    for you,
If you'll only listen a minute, and do as I bid you do.
They'll try to prove me crazy, and, if you bungle, they can;   105
And I've only you to trust to! (O God, why ain't it a man?)
There's some waste money on marbles, the same as M'Cullough
    tried—
Marbles and mausoleums—but I call that sinful pride.
There's some ship bodies for burial—we've carried 'em, soldered
    and packed;
Down in their wills they wrote it, and nobody called *them*
    cracked.   110

But me—I've too much money, and people might . . . All my
    fault:
It come o' hoping for grandsons and buying that Wokin'
    vault. . . .
I'm sick o' the 'ole dam' business. I'm going back where I came.
Dick, you're the son o' my body, and you'll take charge o' the
    same!
I want to lie by your mother, ten thousand mile away,   115
And they'll want to send me to Woking; and that's where you'll
    earn your pay.
I've thought it out on the quiet, the same as it ought to be done—
Quiet, and decent, and proper—an' here's your orders, my son.
You know the Line? You don't, though. You write to the Board,
    and tell
Your father's death has upset you an' you're goin' to cruise for a
    spell,   120
An' you'd like the *Mary Gloster*—I've held her ready for this—
They'll put her in working order and you'll take her out as she is.
Yes, it was money idle when I patched her and laid her aside
(Thank God, I can pay for my fancies!)—the boat where your
    mother died,
By the Little Paternosters, as you come to the Union Bank,   125
We dropped her—I think I told you—and I pricked it off where
    she sank.
['Tiny she looked on the grating—that oily, treacly sea—]
'Hundred and Eighteen East, remember, and South just Three.
Easy bearings to carry—Three South—Three to the dot;
But I gave McAndrew a copy in case of dying—or not.   130
And so you'll write to McAndrew, he's Chief of the Maori Line;
They'll give him leave, if you ask 'em and say it's business o'
    mine.
I built three boats for the Maoris, an' very well pleased they were,
An' I've known Mac since the Fifties, and Mac knew me—and
    her.
After the first stroke warned me I sent him the money to keep   135
Against the time you'd claim it, committin' your dad to the deep;
For you are the son o' my body, and Mac was my oldest friend,
I've never asked 'im to dinner, but he'll see it out to the end.
Stiff-necked Glasgow beggar! I've heard he's prayed for my soul,
But he couldn't lie if you paid him, and he'd starve before he
    stole.   140

He'll take the *Mary* in ballast—you'll find her a lively ship;
And you'll take Sir Anthony Gloster, that goes on 'is wedding-
    trip,
Lashed in our old deck-cabin with all three port-holes wide,
The kick o' the screw beneath him and the round blue seas
    outside!
Sir Anthony Gloster's carriage—our 'ouse-flag flyin' free—   145
Ten thousand men on the pay-roll and forty freighters at sea!
He made himself and a million, but this world is a fleetin' show,
And he'll go to the wife of 'is bosom the same as he ought to go—
By the heel of the Paternosters—there isn't a chance to
    mistake—
And Mac'll pay you the money as soon as the bubbles break!   150
Five thousand for six weeks' cruising, the staunchest freighter
    afloat,
And Mac he'll give you your bonus the minute I'm out o' the
    boat!
He'll take you round to Macassar, and you'll come back alone;
He knows what I want o' the *Mary*. . . . I'll do what I please with
    my own.
Your mother 'ud call it wasteful, but I've seven-and-thirty
    more;   155
I'll come in my private carriage and bid it wait at the door. . . .
For my son 'e was never a credit: 'e muddled with books and art,
And 'e lived on Sir Anthony's money and 'e broke Sir Anthony's
    heart.
There isn't even a grandchild, and the Gloster family's done—
The only one you left me—O mother, the only one!   160
Harrer and Trinity College—me slavin' early an' late—
An' he thinks I'm dying crazy, and you're in Macassar Strait!
Flesh o' my flesh, my dearie, for ever an' ever amen,
That first stroke come for a warning. I ought to ha' gone to you
    then.
But—cheap repairs for a cheap 'un—the doctors said I'd do.   165
Mary, why didn't *you* warn me? I've allus heeded to you,
Excep'—I know—about women; but you are a spirit now;
An', wife, they was only women, and I was a man. That's how.
An' a man 'e must go with a woman, as you *could* not
    understand;
But I never talked 'em secrets. I paid 'em out o' hand.   170

Thank Gawd, I can pay for my fancies! Now what's five thousand
    to me,
For a berth off the Paternosters in the haven where I would be?
I believe in the Resurrection, if I read my Bible plain,
But I wouldn't trust 'em at Wokin'; we're safer at sea again.
For the heart it shall go with the treasure—go down to the sea in
    ships.   175
I'm sick of the hired women. I'll kiss my girl on her lips!
I'll be content with my fountain. I'll drink from my own well,
And the wife of my youth shall charm me—an' the rest can go to
    Hell!
(Dickie, *he* will, that's certain.) I'll lie in our standin'-bed,
An' Mac'll take her in ballast—an' she trims best by the head. . . 180
Down by the head an' sinkin', her fires are drawn and cold,
And the water's splashin' hollow on the skin of the empty hold—
Churning an' choking and chuckling, quiet and scummy and
    dark—
Full to her lower hatches and risin' steady. Hark!
That was the after-bulkhead. . . . She's flooded from stem to
    stern. . . .   185
'Never seen death yet, Dickie? . . . Well, now is your time to learn!

The Liner She's a Lady

The liner she's a lady, an' she never looks nor 'eeds—
The Man-o'-War's 'er 'usband, an' 'e gives 'er all she needs;
But, oh, the little cargo-boats, that sail the wet seas roun',
They're just the same as you an' me a-plyin' up an' down!

    Plyin' up an' down, Jenny, 'angin' round the Yard,   5
    All the way by Fratton tram down to Portsmouth 'Ard;
    Anythin' for business, an' we're growin' old—
    Plyin' up an' down, Jenny, waitin' in the cold!

The Liner she's a lady by the paint upon 'er face,
An' if she meets an accident they count it sore disgrace.   10

The Man-o'-War's 'er 'usband, and 'e's always 'andy by,
But, oh, the little cargo-boats, they've got to load or die!

The Liner she's a lady, and 'er route is cut an' dried;
The Man-o'War's 'er 'usband, an' 'e always keeps beside;
But, oh, the little cargo-boats that 'aven't any man,
They've got to do their business first, and make the most they
    can!

The Liner she's a lady, and if a war should come,
The Man-o'-War's 'er 'usband, and 'e'd bid 'er stay at home;
But, oh, the little cargo-boats that fill with every tide!
'E'd 'ave to up an' fight for them, for they are England's pride.   20

The Liner she's a lady, but if she wasn't made,
There still would be the cargo-boats for 'ome an' foreign trade.
The Man-o'-War's 'er 'usband, but if we wasn't 'ere,
'E wouldn't have to fight at all for 'ome an' friends so dear.

    'Ome an' friends so dear, Jenny, 'angin' round the Yard,
    All the way by Fratton tram down to Portsmouth 'Ard;
    Anythin' for business, an' we're growin' old—
    'Ome an' friends so dear, Jenny, waitin' in the cold!

My Boy Jack

    'Have you news of my boy Jack?'
        Not this tide.
    'When d'you think that he'll come back?'
        Not with this wind blowing, and this tide.

    'Has any one else had word of him?'   5
        Not this tide.
    For what is sunk will hardly swim,
        Not with this wind blowing, and this tide.

'Oh, dear, what comfort can I find?'
>None this tide,   10
>Nor any tide.
Except he did not shame his kind—
>Not even with that wind blowing, and that tide.

Then hold your head up all the more,
>This tide,   15
>And every tide;
Because he was the son you bore,
>And gave to that wind blowing and that tide!

The Vampire

A fool there was and he made his prayer
(Even as you and I!)
To a rag and a bone and a hank of hair
(We called her the woman who did not care)
But the fool he called her his lady fair—   5
(Even as you and I!)

Oh, the years we waste and the tears we waste
And the work of our head and hand
Belong to the woman who did not know
(And now we know that she never could know)   10
And did not understand!

A fool there was and his goods he spent
(Even as you and I!)
Honour and faith and a sure intent
(And it wasn't the least what the lady meant)   15
But a fool must follow his natural bent
(Even as you and I!)

Oh, the toil we lost and the spoil we lost
And the excellent things we planned

Belong to the woman who didn't know why 20
(And now we know that she never knew why)
And did not understand!

The fool was stripped to his foolish hide
(Even as you and I!)
Which she might have seen when she threw him aside— 25
(But it isn't on record the lady tried)
So some of him lived but the most of him died—
(Even as you and I!)

And it isn't the shame and it isn't the blame
That stings like a white-hot brand— 30
It's coming to know that she never knew why
(Seeing, at last, she could never know why)
And never could understand!

The English Flag

Above the portico a flag-staff, bearing the Union Jack, remained
fluttering in the flames for some time, but ultimately when it fell the
crowds rent the air with shouts, and seemed to see significance in the
incident.

DAILY PAPERS

Winds of the World, give answer! They are whimpering to and
    fro—
And what should they know of England who only England
    know?—
The poor little street-bred people that vapour and fume and brag,
They are lifting their heads in the stillness to yelp at the English
    Flag!

Must we borrow a clout from the Boer—to plaster anew with
    dirt? 5

An Irish liar's bandage, or an English coward's shirt?
We may not speak of England; her Flag's to sell or share.
What is the Flag of England? Winds of the World, declare!

The North Wind blew:—'From Bergen my steel-shod vanguards
          go;
'I chase your lazy whalers home from the Disko floe.   10
'By the great North Lights above me I work the will of God,
'And the liner splits on the ice-field or the Dogger fills with cod.

'I barred my gates with iron, I shuttered my doors with flame,
'Because to force my ramparts your nutshell navies came.
'I took the sun from their presence, I cut them down with my
          blast,   15
'And they died, but the Flag of England blew free ere the spirit
          passed.

'The lean white bear hath seen it in the long, long Arctic nights,
'The musk-ox knows the standard that flouts the Northern
          Lights:
'What is the Flag of England? Ye have but my bergs to dare,
'Ye have but my drifts to conquer. Go forth, for it is there!'   20

The South Wind sighed:—'From the Virgins my mid-sea course
          was ta'en
'Over a thousand islands lost in an idle main,
'Where the sea-egg flames on the coral and the long-backed
          breakers croon
'Their endless ocean legends to the lazy, locked lagoon.

'Strayed amid lonely islets, mazed amid outer keys,   25
'I waked the palms to laughter—I tossed the scud in the breeze.
'Never was isle so little, never was sea so lone,
'But over the scud and the palm-trees an English flag was flown.

'I have wrenched it free from the halliards to hang for a wisp on
          the Horn;
'I have chased it north to the Lizard—ribboned and rolled and
          torn;   30
'I have spread its folds o'er the dying, adrift in a hopeless sea;

'I have hurled it swift on the slaver, and seen the slave set free.

'My basking sunfish know it, and wheeling albatross,
'Where the lone wave fills with fire beneath the Southern Cross.
'What is the Flag of England? Ye have but my reefs to dare,   35
'Ye have but my seas to furrow. Go forth, for it is there!'

The East Wind roared:—'From the Kuriles, the Bitter Seas, I
        come,
'And me men call the Home-Wind, for I bring the English home.
'Look—look well to your shipping! By the breath of my mad
        typhoon
'I swept your close-packed Praya and beached your best at
        Kowloon!   40

'The reeling junks behind me and the racing seas before,
'I raped your richest roadstead—I plundered Singapore!
'I set my hand on the Hoogli; as a hooded snake she rose;
'And I flung your stoutest steamers to roost with the startled
        crows.

'Never the lotos closes, never the wild-fowl wake,   45
'But a soul goes out on the East Wind that died for England's
        sake—
'Man or woman or suckling, mother or bride or maid—
'Because on the bones of the English the English Flag is stayed.

'The desert-dust hath dimmed it, the flying wild-ass knows,
'The scared white leopard winds it across the taintless snows.
'What is the Flag of England? Ye have but my sun to dare,   50
'Ye have but my sands to travel. Go forth, for it is there!'

The West Wind called:—'In squadrons the thoughtless galleons
        fly
'That bear the wheat and cattle lest street-bred people die.
'They make my might their porter, they make my house their
        path,   55
'Till I loose my neck from their rudder and whelm them all in my
        wrath.

'I draw the gliding fog-bank as a snake is drawn from the hole.
'They bellow one to the other, the frighted ship-bells toll;
'For day is a drifting terror till I raise the shroud with my breath,

'And they see strange bows above them and the two go locked to
    death.   60

'But whether in calm or wrack-wreath, whether by dark or day,
'I heave them whole to the conger or rip their plates away,
'First of the scattered legions, under a shrieking sky,
'Dipping between the rollers, the English Flag goes by.

'The dead dumb fog hath wrapped it—the frozen dews have
    kissed—   65
'The naked stars have seen it, a fellow-star in the mist.
'What is the Flag of England? Ye have but my breath to dare,
'Ye have but my waves to conquer. Go forth, for it is there!'

The Ballad of East and West

Oh, East is East, and West is West, and never the twain shall meet,
Till Earth and Sky stand presently at God's great Judgment Seat;
But there is neither East nor West, Border, nor Breed, nor Birth,
When two strong men stand face to face, though they come from the
    ends of the earth!

Kamal is out with twenty men to raise the Border-side,   5
And he has lifted the Colonel's mare that is the Colonel's pride.
He has lifted her out of the stable-door between the dawn and the
    day,
And turned the calkins upon her feet, and ridden her far away.
Then up and spoke the Colonel's son that led a troop of the
    Guides:
'Is there never a man of all my men can say where Kamal hides?'
Then up and spoke Mohammed Khan, the son of the Ressaldar:
'If ye know the track of the morning-mist, ye know where his
    pickets are.
'At dusk he harries the Abazai—at dawn he is into Bonair,
'But he must go by Fort Bukloh to his own place to fare.
'So if ye gallop to Fort Bukloh as fast as a bird can fly,   15

'By the favour of God ye may cut him off ere he win to the
          Tongue of Jagai.
'But if he be past the Tongue of Jagai, right swiftly turn ye then,
'For the length and the breadth of that grisly plain is sown with
          Kamal's men.
'There is rock to the left, and rock to the right, and low lean
          thorn between,
'And ye may hear a breech-bolt snick where never a man is
          seen.'   20
The Colonel's son has taken horse, and a raw rough dun was he,
With the mouth of a bell and the heart of Hell and the head of a
          gallows-tree.
The Colonel's son to the Fort has won, they bid him stay to eat—
Who rides at the tail of a Border thief, he sits not long at his meat.
He's up and away from Fort Bukloh as fast as he can fly,   25
Till he was aware of his father's mare in the gut of the Tongue of
          Jagai,
Till he was aware of his father's mare with Kamal upon her back,
And when he could spy the white of her eye, he made the pistol
          crack.
He has fired once, he has fired twice, but the whistling ball went
          wide.
'Ye shoot like a soldier,' Kamal said. 'Show now if ye can ride!' 30
It's up and over the Tongue of Jagai, as blown dust-devils go,
The dun he fled like a stag of ten, but the mare like a barren doe.
The dun he leaned against the bit and slugged his head above,
But the red mare played with the snaffle-bars, as a maiden plays
          with a glove.
There was rock to the left and rock to the right, and low lean
          thorn between,   35
And thrice he heard a breech-bolt snick tho' never a man was
          seen.
They have ridden the low moon out of the sky, their hoofs drum
          up the dawn,
The dun he went like a wounded bull, but the mare like a new-
          roused fawn.
The dun he fell at a water-course—in a woeful heap fell he,
And Kamal has turned the red mare back, and pulled the rider
          free.   40
He has knocked the pistol out of his hand—small room was there
          to strive,

' 'Twas only by favour of mine,' quoth he, 'ye rode so long alive:
'There was not a rock for twenty mile, there was not a clump of
     tree,
'But covered a man of my own men with his rifle cocked on his
     knee.
'If I had raised my bridle-hand, as I have held it low,   45
'The little jackals that flee so fast were feasting all in a row,
'If I had bowed my head on my breast, as I have held it high,
'The kite that whistles above us now were gorged till she could
     not fly.'
Lightly answered the Colonel's son: 'Do good to bird and beast,
'But count who come for the broken meats before thou makest a
     feast.   50
'If there should follow a thousand swords to carry my bones
     away,
'Belike the price of a jackal's meal were more than a thief could
     pay.
'They will feed their horse on the standing crop, their men on the
     garnered grain.
'The thatch of the byres will serve their fires when all the cattle
     are slain.
'But if thou thinkest the price be fair,—thy brethren wait to sup,
'The hound is kin to the jackal-spawn,—howl, dog, and call them
     up!
'And if thou thinkest the price be high, in steer and gear and
     stack,
'Give me my father's mare again, and I'll fight my own way
     back!'
Kamal has gripped him by the hand and set him upon his feet.
'No talk shall be of dogs,' said he, 'when wolf and grey wolf meet.
'May I eat dirt if thou hast hurt of me in deed or breath;
'What dam of lances brought thee forth to jest at the dawn with
     Death?'
Lightly answered the Colonel's son: 'I hold by the blood of my
     clan:
'Take up the mare for my father's gift—by God, she has carried a
     man!'
The red mare ran to the Colonel's son, and nuzzled against his
     breast;   65

'We be two strong men,' said Kamal then, 'but she loveth the
     younger best.
'So she shall go with a lifter's dower, my turquoise-studded rein,
'My 'broidered saddle and saddle-cloth, and silver stirrups twain.'
The Colonel's son a pistol drew, and held it muzzle-end,
'Ye have taken the one from a foe,' said he. 'Will ye take the mate
     from a friend?'   70
'A gift for a gift,' said Kamal straight; 'a limb for the risk of a limb.
'Thy father has sent his son to me, I'll send my son to him!'
With that he whistled his only son, that dropped from a
     mountain-crest—
He trod the ling like a buck in spring, and he looked like a lance
     in rest.
'Now here is thy master,' Kamal said, 'who leads a troop of the
     Guides,   75
'And thou must ride at his left side as shield on shoulder rides.
'Till Death or I cut loose the tie, at camp and board and bed,
'Thy life is his—thy fate it is to guard him with thy head.
'So, thou must eat the White Queen's meat, and all her foes are
     thine,
'And thou must harry thy father's hold for the peace of the
     Border-line.   80
'And thou must make a trooper tough and hack thy way to
     power—
'Belike they will raise thee to Ressaldar when I am hanged in
     Peshawur!'

They have looked each other between the eyes, and there they
     found no fault.
They have taken the Oath of the Brother-in-Blood on leavened
     bread and salt:
They have taken the Oath of the Brother-in-Blood on fire and
     fresh-cut sod,   85
On the hilt and the haft of the Khyber knife, and the Wondrous
     Names of God.
The Colonel's son he rides the mare and Kamal's boy the dun,
And two have come back to Fort Bukloh where there went forth
     but one.
And when they drew to the Quarter-Guard, full twenty swords
     flew clear—

There was not a man but carried his feud with the blood of the
    mountaineer.   90
'Ha' done! ha' done!' said the Colonel's son. 'Put up the steel at
    your sides!
'Last night ye had struck at a Border thief—to-night 'tis a man of
    the Guides!'

Oh, East is East, and West is West, and never the twain shall meet,
Till Earth and Sky stand presently at God's great Judgment Seat;
But there is neither East nor West, Border, nor Breed, nor Birth,   95
When two strong men stand face to face, though they come from the
    ends of the earth!

Gehazi

Whence comest thou, Gehazi,
    So reverend to behold,
In scarlet and in ermines
    And chain of England's gold?
'From following after Naaman   5
    To tell him all is well,
Whereby my zeal hath made me
    A Judge in Israel.'

Well done, well done, Gehazi!
    Stretch forth thy ready hand.   10
Thou barely 'scaped from judgment,
    Take oath to judge the land
Unswayed by gift of money
    Or privy bribe, more base,
Of knowledge which is profit   15
    In any market-place.

Search out and probe, Gehazi,
    As thou of all canst try,
The truthful, well-weighed answer
    That tells the blacker lie—   20

The loud, uneasy virtue,
    The anger feigned at will,
To overbear a witness
    And make the Court keep still.

Take order now, Gehazi,   25
    That no man talk aside
In secret with his judges
    The while his case is tried.
Lest he should show them—reason
    To keep a matter hid,   30
And subtly lead the questions
    Away from that he did.

Thou mirror of uprightness,
    What ails thee at thy vows?
What means the risen whiteness   35
    Of the skin between thy brows?
The boils that shine and burrow,
    The sores that slough and bleed—
The leprosy of Naaman
    On thee and all thy seed?   40
        Stand up, stand up, Gehazi,
            Draw close thy robe and go,
        Gehazi, Judge in Israel,
            A leper white as snow!

The Islanders

No doubt but ye are the People—your throne is above the King's.
Whoso speaks in your presence must say acceptable things:
Bowing the head in worship, bending the knee in fear—
Bringing the word well smoothen—such as a King should hear.

Fenced by your careful fathers, ringed by your leaden seas,   5
Long did ye wake in quiet and long lie down at ease;

Till ye said of Strife, 'What is it?' of the Sword, 'It is far from our
    ken';
Till ye made a sport of your shrunken hosts and a toy of your
    armèd men.
Ye stopped your ears to the warning—ye would neither look nor
    heed—
Ye set your leisure before their toil and your lusts above their
    need.   10
Because of your witless learning and your beasts of warren and
    chase,
Ye grudged your sons to their service and your fields for their
    camping-place.
Ye forced them glean in the highways the straw for the bricks
    they brought;
Ye forced them follow in byways the craft that ye never taught.
Ye hampered and hindered and crippled; yet thrust out of sight
    and away   15
Those that would serve you for honour and those that served you
    for pay.
Then were the judgments loosened; then was your shame
    revealed,
At the hands of a little people, few but apt in the field.
Yet ye were saved by a remnant (and your land's long-suffering
    star),
When your strong men cheered in their millions while your
    striplings went to the war.   20
Sons of the sheltered city—unmade, unhandled, unmeet—
Ye pushed them raw to the battle as ye picked them raw from the
    street.
And what did ye look they should compass? Warcraft learned in
    a breath,
Knowledge unto occasion at the first far view of Death?
So? And ye train your horses and the dogs ye feed and prize?   25
How are the beasts more worthy than the souls, your sacrifice?
But ye said, 'Their valour shall show them'; but ye said, 'The end
    is close.'
And ye sent them comfits and pictures to help them harry your
    foes:
And ye vaunted your fathomless power, and ye flaunted your
    iron pride,

Ere—ye fawned on the Younger Nations for the men who could
    shoot and ride!   30
Then ye returned to your trinkets; then ye contented your souls
With the flannelled fools at the wicket or the muddied oafs at the
    goals.
Given to strong delusion, wholly believing a lie,
Ye saw that the land lay fenceless, and ye let the months go by
Waiting some easy wonder, hoping some saving sign—   35
Idle—openly idle—in the lee of the forespent Line.
Idle—except for your boasting—and what is your boasting worth
If ye grudge a year of service to the lordliest life on earth?
Ancient, effortless, ordered, cycle on cycle set,
Life so long untroubled, that ye who inherit forget   40
It was not made with the mountains, it is not one with the deep.
Men, not gods, devised it. Men, not gods, must keep.
Men, not children, servants, or kinsfolk called from afar,
But each man born in the Island broke to the matter of war.
Soberly and by custom taken and trained for the same,   45
Each man born in the Island entered at youth to the game—
As it were almost cricket, not to be mastered in haste,
But after trial and labour, by temperance, living chaste.
As it were almost cricket—as it were even your play,
Weighed and pondered and worshipped, and practised day and
    day.   50
So ye shall bide sure-guarded when the restless lightnings wake
In the womb of the blotting war-cloud, and the pallid nations
    quake.
So, at the haggard trumpets, instant your soul shall leap
Forthright, accoutred, accepting—alert from the wells of sleep.
So at the threat ye shall summon—so at the need ye shall send 55
Men, not children or servants, tempered and taught to the end,
Cleansed of servile panic, slow to dread or despise,
Humble because of knowledge, mighty by sacrifice. . . .
But ye say, 'It will mar our comfort.' Ye say, 'It will minish our
    trade.'
Do ye wait for the spattered shrapnel ere ye learn how a gun is
    laid?   60
For the low, red glare to southward when the raided coast-towns
    burn?
(Light ye shall have on that lesson, but little time to learn.)

Will ye pitch some white pavilion, and lustily even the odds,
With nets and hoops and mallets, with rackets and bats and rods?
Will the rabbit war with your foemen—the red deer horn them
    for hire? 65
Your kept cock-pheasant keep you?—he is master of many a
    shire.
Arid, aloof, incurious, unthinking, unthanking, gelt,
Will ye loose your schools to flout them till their brow-beat
    columns melt?
Will ye pray them or preach them, or print them, or ballot them
    back from your shore?
Will your workmen issue a mandate to bid them strike no more?
Will ye rise and dethrone your rulers? (Because ye were idle both?
Pride by Insolence chastened? Indolence purged by Sloth?)
No doubt but ye are the People; who shall make you afraid?
Also your gods are many; no doubt but your gods shall aid.
Idols of greasy altars built for the body's ease; 75
Proud little brazen Baals and talking fetishes;
Teraphs of sept and party and wise wood-pavement gods—
These shall come down to the battle and snatch you from under
    the rods?
From the gusty, flickering gun-roll with viewless salvoes rent,
And the pitted hail of the bullets that tell not whence they were
    sent. 80
When ye are ringed as with iron, when ye are scourged as with
    whips,
When the meat is yet in your belly, and the boast is yet on your
    lips;
When ye go forth at morning and the noon beholds you broke,
Ere ye lie down at even, your remnant, under the yoke?

No doubt but ye are the People—absolute, strong, and wise; 85
Whatever your heart has desired ye have not withheld from your eyes.
On your own heads, in your own hands, the sin and the saving lies!

The White Man's Burden

(The United States and the Philippine Islands)

Take up the White Man's Burden—
    Send forth the best ye breed—
Go bind your sons to exile
    To serve your captives' need;
To wait in heavy harness   5
    On fluttered folk and wild—
Your new-caught, sullen peoples,
    Half devil and half child.

Take up the White Man's Burden—
    In patience to abide,   10
To veil the threat of terror
    And check the show of pride;
By open speech and simple,
    An hundred times made plain,
To seek another's profit,   15
    And work another's gain.

Take up the White Man's burden—
    The savage wars of peace—
Fill full the mouth of Famine
    And bid the sickness cease;   20
And when your goal is nearest
    The end for others sought,
Watch Sloth and heathen Folly
    Bring all your hope to nought.

Take up the White Man's burden—   25
    No tawdry rule of kings,
But toil of serf and sweeper—
    The tale of common things.
The ports ye shall not enter,
    The roads ye shall not tread,   30
Go makē them with your living,
    And mark them with your dead!

Take up the White Man's burden—
    And reap his old reward:
The blame of those ye better,   35
    The hate of those ye guard—
The cry of hosts ye humour
    (Ah, slowly!) toward the light:–
'Why brought ye us from bondage,
    'Our loved Egyptian night?'   40

Take up the White Man's burden—
    Ye dare not stoop to less—
Nor call too loud on Freedom
    To cloak your weariness;
By all ye cry or whisper,   45
    By all ye leave or do,
The silent, sullen peoples
    Shall weigh your Gods and you.

Take up the White Man's burden—
    Have done with childish days—   50
The lightly proffered laurel,
    The easy, ungrudged praise.
Comes now, to search your manhood
    Through all the thankless years,
Cold-edged with dear-bought wisdom,   55
    The judgment of your peers!

Recessional

God of our fathers, known of old,
    Lord of our far-flung battle-line,
Beneath whose awful Hand we hold
    Dominion over palm and pine—
Lord God of Hosts, be with us yet,   5
Lest we forget—lest we forget!

The tumult and the shouting dies;
 The Captains and the Kings depart:
Still Stands Thine ancient sacrifice,
 An humble and a contrite heart.   10
Lord God of Hosts, be with us yet,
Lest we forget—lest we forget!

Far-called, our navies melt away;
 On dune and headland sinks the fire:
Lo, all our pomp of yesterday   15
 Is one with Nineveh and Tyre!
Judge of the Nations, spare us yet,
Lest we forget—lest we forget!

If, drunk with sight of power, we loose
 Wild tongues that have not Thee in awe, 20
Such boastings as the Gentiles use,
 Or lesser breeds without the Law—
Lord God of Hosts, be with us yet,
Lest we forget—lest we forget!

For heathen heart that puts her trust   25
 In reeking tube and iron shard,
All valiant dust that builds on dust,
 And guarding, calls not Thee to guard,
For frantic boast and foolish word—
Thy mercy on Thy People, Lord!   30

The Three-Decker

'The three-volume novel is extinct.'

Full thirty foot she towered from waterline to rail.
It took a watch to steer her, and a week to shorten sail;
But, spite all modern notions, I've found her first and best—
The only certain packet for the Islands of the Blest.

Fair held the breeze behind us—'twas warm with lovers' prayers.5
We'd stolen wills for ballast and a crew of missing heirs.
They shipped as Able Bastards till the Wicked Nurse confessed,
And they worked the old three-decker to the Islands of the Blest.

By ways no gaze could follow, a course unspoiled of Cook,
Per Fancy, fleetest in man, our titled berths we took   10
With maids of matchless beauty and parentage unguessed,
And a Church of England parson for the Islands of the Blest.

We asked no social questions—we pumped no hidden shame—
We never talked obstetrics when the Little Stranger came:
We left the Lord in Heaven, we left the fiends in Hell.   15
We weren't exactly Yussufs, but—Zuleika didn't tell.

No moral doubt assailed us, so when the port we neared,
The villain had his flogging at the gangway, and we cheered.
'Twas fiddle in the foc's'le—'twas garlands on the mast,
For every one got married, and I went ashore at last.   20

I left 'em all in couples a-kissing on the decks.
I left the lovers loving and the parents signing cheques.
In endless English comfort, by county-folk caressed,
I left the old three-decker at the Islands of the Blest! . . .

That route is barred to steamers: you'll never lift again   25
Our purple-painted headlands or the lordly keeps of Spain.
They're just beyond your skyline, howe'er so far you cruise
In a ram-you-damn-you liner with a brace of bucking screws.

Swing round your aching searchlight—'twill show no haven's
      peace.
Ay, blow your shrieking sirens at the deaf, grey-bearded seas!   30
Boom out the dripping oil-bags to skin the deep's unrest—
And you aren't one knot the nearer to the Islands of the Blest.

But when you're threshing, crippled, with broken bridge and rail,
At a drogue of dead convictions to hold you head to gale,
Calm as the Flying Dutchman, from truck to taffrail dressed,   35
You'll see the old three-decker for the Islands of the Blest.

You'll see her tiering canvas in sheeted silver spread;
You'll hear the long-drawn thunder 'neath her leaping figure-
          head;
While far, so far above you, her tall poop-lanterns shine
Unvexed by wind or weather like the candles round a shrine!   40

Hull down—hull down and under—she dwindles to a speck,
With noise of pleasant music and dancing on her deck.
All's well—all's well aboard her—she's left you far behind,
With a scent of old-world roses through the fog that ties you
          blind.

Her crews are babes or madmen? Her port is all to make?   45
You're manned by Truth and Science, and you steam for
          steaming's sake?
Well, tinker up your engines—you know your business best—
She's taking tired people to the Islands of the Blest!

The Conundrum of the Workshops

When the flush of a new-born sun fell first on Eden's green and
          gold,
Our father Adam sat under the Tree and scratched with a stick in
          the mould;
And the first rude sketch that the world had seen was joy to his
          mighty heart,
Till the Devil whispered behind the leaves, 'It's pretty, but is it
          Art?'

Wherefore he called to his wife, and fled to fashion his work
          anew—   5
The first of his race who cared a fig for the first, most dread
          review;
And he left his lore to the use of his sons—and that was a
          glorious gain

When the Devil chuckled 'Is it Art?' in the ear of the branded
    Cain.

They builded a tower to shiver the sky and wrench the stars
    apart,
Till the Devil grunted behind the bricks: 'It's striking, but is it
    Art?'   10
The stone was dropped at the quarry-side and the idle derrick
    swung,
While each man talked of the aims of Art, and each in an alien
    tongue.

They fought and they talked in the North and the South; they
    talked and they fought in the West,
Till the waters rose on the pitiful land, and the poor Red Clay had
    rest—
Had rest till that dank blank-canvas dawn when the Dove was
    preened to start,   15
And the Devil bubbled below the keel: 'It's human, but is it Art?'

The tale is as old as the Eden Tree—and new as the new-cut
    tooth—
For each man knows ere his lip-thatch grows he is master of Art
    and Truth;
And each man hears as the twilight nears, to the beat of his
    dying heart,
The Devil drum on the darkened pane: 'You did it, but was it
    Art?'   20

We have learned to whittle the Eden Tree to the shape of a
    surplice-peg,
We have learned to bottle our parents twain in the yelk of an
    addled egg,
We know that the tail must wag the dog, for the horse is drawn
    by the cart;
But the Devil whoops, as he whooped of old: 'It's clever, but is it
    Art?'

When the flicker of London sun falls faint on the Clubroom's
    green and gold,   25

The sons of Adam sit them down and scratch with their pens in
    the mould—
They scratch with their pens in the mould of their graves, and
    the ink and the anguish start,
For the Devil mutters behind the leaves: 'It's pretty, but is it Art?'

Now, if we could win to the Eden Tree where the Four Great
    Rivers flow,
And the Wreath of Eve is red on the turf as she left it long ago, 30
And if we could come when the sentry slept and softly scurry
    through,
By the favour of God we might know as much—as our father
    Adam knew!

The Benefactors

Ah! What avails the classic bent
    And what the cultured word,
Against the undoctored incident
    That actually occurred?

And what is Art whereto we press   5
    Through paint and prose and rhyme—
When Nature in her nakedness
    Defeats us every time?

It is not learning, grace nor gear,
    Nor easy meat and drink,   10
But bitter pinch of pain and fear
    That makes creation think.

When in this world's unpleasing youth
    Our godlike race began,
The longest arm, the sharpest tooth,   15
    Gave man control of man;

Till, bruised and bitten to the bone
    And taught by pain and fear,
He learned to deal the far-off stone,
    And poke the long, safe spear.   20

So tooth and nail were obsolete
    As means against a foe,
Till, bored by uniform defeat,
    Some genius built the bow.

Then stone and javelin proved as vain   25
    As old-time tooth and nail;
Till, spurred anew by fear and pain,
    Man fashioned coats of mail.

Then was there safety for the rich
    And danger for the poor,   30
Till someone mixed a powder which
    Redressed the scale once more.

Helmet and armour disappeared
    With sword and bow and pike,
And, when the smoke of battle cleared,   35
    All men were armed alike. . . .

And when ten million such were slain
    To please one crazy king,
Man, schooled in bulk by fear and pain,
    Grew weary of the thing: 40.

And, at the very hour designed
    To enslave him past recall,
His tooth-stone-arrow-gun-shy mind
    Turned and abolished all.

All Power, each Tyrant, every Mob   45
    Whose head has grown too large,
Ends by destroying its own job
    And works its own discharge;

And Man, whose mere necessities
    Move all things from his path,   50
Trembles meanwhile at their decrees,
    And deprecates their wrath!

When 'Omer Smote 'is Bloomin' Lyre

(Introduction to the Barrack-Room Ballads in
'The Seven Seas')

When 'Omer smote 'is bloomin' lyre,
    He'd 'eard men sing by land an' sea;
An' what he thought 'e might require,
    'E went an' took—the same as me!

The market-girls an' fishermen,   5
    The shepherds an' the sailors, too,
They 'eard old songs turn up again,
    But kep' it quiet—same as you!

They knew 'e stole; 'e knew they knowed.
    They didn't tell, nor make a fuss,   10
But winked at 'Omer down the road,
    An' 'e winked back—the same as us!

Tomlinson

Now Tomlinson gave up the ghost at his house in Berkeley
        Square,
And a Spirit came to his bedside and gripped him by the hair—
A Spirit gripped him by the hair and carried him far away,
Till he heard as the roar of a rain-fed ford the roar of the Milky
        Way:
Till he heard the roar of the Milky Way die down and drone and
        cease,   5
And they came to the Gate within the Wall where Peter holds the
        keys.
'Stand up, stand up now, Tomlinson, and answer loud and high
'The good that ye did for the sake of men or ever ye came to die—
'The good that ye did for the sake of men on little Earth so lone!'

And the naked soul of Tomlinson grew white as a rainwashed
    bone.   10
'O I have a friend on Earth,' he said, 'that was my priest and
    guide,
'And well would he answer all for me if he were at my side.'
—'For that ye strove in neighbour-love it shall be written fair,
'But now ye wait at Heaven's Gate and not in Berkeley Square:
'Though we called your friend from his bed this night, he could
    not speak for you,   15
'For the race is run by one and one and never by two and two.'
Then Tomlinson looked up and down, and little gain was there,
For the naked stars grinned overhead, and he saw that his soul
    was bare.
The Wind that blows between the Worlds, it cut him like a knife,
And Tomlinson took up the tale and spoke of his good in life.   20
'O this I have read in a book,' he said, 'and that was told to me,
'And this I have thought that another man thought of a Prince in
    Muscovy.'
The good souls flocked like homing doves and bade him clear the
    path,
And Peter twirled the jangling Keys in weariness and wrath.
'Ye have read, ye have heard, ye have thought,' he said, 'and the
    tale is yet to run: 25
'By the worth of the body that once ye had, give answer— what
    ha' ye done?'
Then Tomlinson looked back and forth, and little good it bore,
For the darkness stayed at his shoulder-blade and Heaven's Gate
    before:—
'O this I have felt, and this I have guessed, and this I have heard
    men say,
'And this they wrote that another man wrote of a carl in
    Norroway.'   30
'Ye have read, ye have felt, ye have guessed, good lack! Ye have
    hampered Heaven's Gate;
'There's little room between the stars in idleness to prate!
'For none may reach by hired speech of neighbour, priest, and
    kin
'Through borrowed deed to God's good meed that lies so fair
    within;

'Get hence, get hence to the Lord of Wrong, for the doom has yet
    to run,   35
'And . . . the faith that ye share with Berkeley Square uphold
    you, Tomlinson!'

The Spirit gripped him by the hair, and sun by sun they fell
Till they came to the belt of Naughty Stars that rim the mouth of
    Hell.
The first are red with pride and wrath, the next are white with
    pain,
But the third are black with clinkered sin that cannot burn again.
They may hold their path, they may leave their path, with never
    a soul to mark:
They may burn or freeze, but they must not cease in the Scorn of
    the Outer Dark.
The Wind that blows between the Worlds, it nipped him to the
    bone,
And he yearned to the flare of Hell-gate there as the light of his
    own hearth-stone.
The Devil he sat behind the bars, where the desperate legions
    drew,   45
But he caught the hasting Tomlinson and would not let him
    through.
'Wot ye the price of good pit-coal that I must pay?' said he,
'That ye rank yoursel' so fit for Hell and ask no leave of me?
'I am all o'er-sib to Adam's breed that ye should give me scorn,
'For I strove with God for your First Father the day that he was
    born.   50
'Sit down, sit down upon the slag, and answer loud and high
'The harm that ye did to the Sons of Men or ever you came to
    die.'
And Tomlinson looked up and up, and saw against the night
The belly of a tortured star blood-red in Hell-Mouth light;
And Tomlinson looked down and down, and saw beneath his feet
The frontlet of a tortured star milk-white in Hell-Mouth heat.
'O I had a love on earth,' said he, 'that kissed me to my fall;
'And if ye would call my love to me I know she would answer
    all.'
—'All that ye did in love forbid it shall be written fair,
'But now ye wait at Hell-Mouth Gate and not in Berkeley Square:

'Though we whistled your love from her bed to-night, I trow she
would not run,
'For the sin ye do by two and two ye must pay for one by one!'
The Wind that blows between the Worlds, it cut him like a knife,
And Tomlinson took up the tale and spoke of his sins in life:—
'Once I ha' laughed at the power of Love and twice at the grip of
the Grave   65
'And thrice I ha' patted my God on the head that men might call
me brave.'
The Devil he blew on a brandered soul and set it aside to cool:—
'Do ye think I would waste my good pit-coal on the hide of a
brain-sick fool?
'I see no worth in the hobnailed mirth or the jolthead jest ye did
'That I should waken my gentlemen that are sleeping three on a
grid.'   70
Then Tomlinson looked back and forth, and there was little
grace,
For Hell-Gate filled the houseless soul with the Fear of Naked
Space.
'Nay, this I ha' heard,' quo' Tomlinson, 'and this was noised
abroad,
'And this I ha' got from a Belgian book on the word of a dead
French lord.'
—'Ye ha' heard, ye ha' read, ye ha' got, good lack! and the tale
begins afresh—   75
'Have ye sinned one sin for the pride o' the eye or the sinful lust
of the flesh?'
Then Tomlinson he gripped the bars and yammered, 'Let me in—
'For I mind that I borrowed my neighbour's wife to sin the deadly
sin.'
The Devil he grinned behind the bars, and banked the fires high:
'Did ye read of that sin in a book?' said he; and Tomlinson said,
'Ay!'   80
The Devil he blew upon his nails, and the little-devils ran,
And he said: 'Go husk this whimpering thief that comes in the
guise of a man:
'Winnow him out 'twixt star and star, and sieve his proper
worth:
'There's sore decline in Adam's line if this be spawn of Earth.'
Empusa's crew, so naked-new they may not face the fire,   85

But weep that they bin too small to sin to the height of their
　　　desire,
Over the coal they chased the Soul, and racked it all abroad;
As children rifle a caddis-case or the raven's foolish hoard.
And back they came with the tattered Thing, as children after
　　　play,
And they said: 'The soul that he got from God he has bartered
　　　clean away.   90
'We have threshed a stook of print and book, and winnowed a
　　　chattering wind,
'And many a soul wherefrom he stole, but his we cannot find.
'We have handled him, we have dandled him, we have seared
　　　him to the bone,
'And, Sire, if tooth and nail show truth he has no soul of his
　　　own.'
The Devil he bowed his head on his breast and rumbled deep and
　　　low:—   95
'I'm all o'er-sib to Adam's breed that I should bid him go.
'Yet close we lie, and deep we lie, and if I gave him place,
'My gentlemen that are so proud would flout me to my face;
'They'd call my house a common stews and me a careless host,
'And—I would not anger my gentlemen for the sake of a shiftless
　　　ghost.'   100
The Devil he looked at the mangled Soul that prayed to feel the
　　　flame,
And he thought of Holy Charity, but he thought of his own good
　　　name:—
'Now ye could haste my coal to waste, and sit ye down to fry.
'Did ye think of that theft for yourself?' said he; and Tomlinson
　　　said, 'Ay!'
The Devil he blew an outward breath, for his heart was free from
　　　care:—   105
'Ye have scarce the soul of a louse,' he said, 'but the roots of sin
　　　are there,
'And for that sin should ye come in were I the lord alone,
'But sinful pride has rule inside—ay, mightier than my own.
'Honour and Wit, fore-damned they sit, to each his Priest and
　　　Whore;
'Nay, scarce I dare myself go there, and you they'd torture sore.

'Ye are neither spirit nor spirk,' he said; 'ye are neither book nor
    brute—
'Go, get ye back to the flesh again for the sake of Man's repute.
'I'm all o'er-sib to Adam's breed that I should mock your pain,
'But look that ye win to worthier sin ere ye come back again.
'Get hence, the hearse is at your door—the grim black stallions
    wait   115
'They bear your clay to place to-day. Speed, lest ye come too late!
'Go back to Earth with a lip unsealed—go back with an open eye,
'And carry my word to the Sons of Men or ever ye come to die;
'That the sin they do by two and two they must pay for one by
    one,
'And . . . the God that you took from a printed book be with you,
    Tomlinson!'   120

The Female of the Species

When the Himalayan peasant meets the he-bear in his pride,
He shouts to scare the monster, who will often turn aside.
But the she-bear thus accosted rends the peasant tooth and nail.
For the female of the species is more deadly than the male.

When Nag the basking cobra hears the careless foot of man,   5
He will sometimes wriggle sideways and avoid it if he can.
But his mate makes no such motion where she camps beside the
    trail.
For the female of the species is more deadly than the male.

When the early Jesuit fathers preached to Hurons and Choctaws,
They prayed to be delivered from the vengeance of the squaws. 10
'Twas the women, not the warriors, turned those dark
    enthusiasts pale.
For the female of the species is more deadly than the male.

Man's timid heart is bursting with the things he must not say,
For the Woman that God gave him isn't his to give away:

But when hunter meets with husband, each confirms the other's
    tale—   15
The female of the species is more deadly than the male.

Man, a bear in most relations—worm and savage otherwise,—
Man propounds negotiations, Man accepts the compromise.
Very rarely will he squarely push the logic of a fact
To its ultimate conclusion in unmitigated act.   20

Fear, or foolishness, impels him, ere he lay the wicked low,
To concede some form of trial even to his fiercest foe.
Mirth obscene diverts his anger—Doubt and Pity oft perplex
Him in dealing with an issue—to the scandal of The Sex!

But the Woman that God gave him, every fibre of her frame   25
Proves her launched for one sole issue, armed and engined for
    the same;
And to serve that single issue, lest the generations fail,
The female of the species must be deadlier than the male.

She who faces Death by torture for each life beneath her breast
May not deal in doubt or pity—must not swerve for fact or jest. 30
These be purely male diversions—not in these her honour dwells.
She the Other Law we live by, is that Law and nothing else.

She can bring no more to living than the powers that make her
    great
As the Mother of the Infant and the Mistress of the Mate.
And when Babe and Man are lacking and she strides unclaimed
    to claim   35
Her right as femme (and baron), her equipment is the same.

She is wedded to convictions—in default of grosser ties;
Her contentions are her children, Heaven help him who denies!—
He will meet no suave discussion, but the instant, white-hot,
    wild,
Wakened female of the species warring as for spouse and child. 40

Unprovoked and awful charges—even so the she-bear fights,
Speech that drips, corrodes, and poisons—even so the cobra bites,
Scientific vivisection of one nerve till it is raw

And the victim writhes in anguish—like the Jesuit with the
    squaw!

So it comes that Man, the coward, when he gathers to confer   45
With his fellow-braves in council, dare not leave a place for her
Where, at war with Life and Conscience, he uplifts his erring
    hands
To some God of Abstract Justice—which no woman understands.

And Man knows it! Knows, moreover, that the Woman that God
    gave him
Must command but may not govern—shall enthral but not
    enslave him.   50
And *She* knows, because She warns him, and Her instincts never
    fail,
That the Female of Her Species is more deadly than the Male.

The Sons of Martha

The Sons of Mary seldom bother, for they have inherited that good
    part;
But the Sons of Martha favour their Mother of the careful soul and
    the troubled heart.
And because she lost her temper once, and because she was rude to
    the Lord her Guest,
Her Sons must wait upon Mary's Sons, world without end, reprieve,
    or rest.

It is their care in all the ages to take the buffet and cushion the
    shock.   5
It is their care that the gear engages; it is their care that the switches
    lock.
It is their care that the wheels run truly; it is their care to embark
    and entrain,
Tally, transport, and deliver duly the Sons of Mary by land and
    main.

They say to mountains, 'Be ye removèd.' They say to the lesser
    floods, 'Be dry.'
Under their rods are the rocks reprovèd—they are not afraid of
    that which is high.   10
Then do the hill-tops shake to the summit—then is the bed of the
    deep laid bare,
That the Sons of Mary may overcome it, pleasantly sleeping and
    unaware.

They finger death at their gloves' end where they piece and repiece
    the living wires.
He rears against the gates they tend: they feed him hungry behind
    their fires.
Early at dawn, ere men see clear, they stumble into his terrible
    stall,   15
And hale him forth like a haltered steer, and goad and turn him till
    evenfall.

To these from birth is Belief forbidden; from these till death is Relief
    afar.
They are concerned with matters hidden—under the earth-line
    their altars are—
The secret fountains to follow up, waters withdrawn to restore to
    the mouth,
And gather the floods as in a cup, and pour them again at a city's
    drouth.   20

They do not preach that their God will rouse them a little before the
    nuts work loose.
They do not teach that His Pity allows them to drop their job when
    they dam'-well choose.
As in the thronged and the lighted ways, so in the dark and the
    desert they stand,
Wary and watchful all their days that their brethren's days may be
    long in the land.

Raise ye the stone or cleave the wood to make a path more fair or
    flat—   25
Lo, it is black already with blood some Son of Martha spilled for
    that!
Not as a ladder from earth to Heaven, not as a witness to any creed,

But simple service simply given to his own kind in their common
need.

And the sons of Mary smile and are blessèd—they know the Angels
are on their side.
They know in them is the Grace confessèd, and for them are the
Mercies multiplied.   30
They sit at the Feet—they hear the Word—they see how truly the
Promise runs.
They have cast their burden upon the Lord, and—the Lord He lays
it on Martha's Sons!

Danny Deever

'What are the bugles blowin' for?' said Files-on-Parade.
'To turn you out, to turn you out,' the Colour-Sergeant said.
'What makes you look so white, so white?' said Files-on-Parade.
'I'm dreadin' what I've got to watch,' the Colour-Sergeant said.
    For they're hangin' Danny Deever, you can hear the Dead
      March play,   5
    The Regiment's in 'ollow square—they're hangin' him to-day;
    They've taken of his buttons off an' cut his stripes away,
    An' they're hangin' Danny Deever in the mornin'.

'What makes the rear-rank breathe so 'ard?' said Files-on-Parade.
'It's bitter cold, it's bitter cold,' the Colour-Sergeant said.   10
'What makes that front-rank man fall down?' said Files-on-
    Parade.
'A touch o' sun, a touch o' sun,' the Colour-Sergeant said.
    They are hangin' Danny Deever, they are marchin' of 'im
      round,
    They 'ave 'alted Danny Deever by 'is coffin on the ground:
    An' 'e'll swing in 'arf a minute for a sneakin' shootin'
      hound—   15
    O they're hangin' Danny Deever in the mornin'!

' 'Is cot was right-' and cot to mine,' said Files-on-Parade.
' 'E's sleepin' out an' far tonight,' the Colour-Sergeant said.
'I've drunk 'is beer a score o' times,' said Files-on-Parade.
' 'E's drinkin' bitter beer alone,' the Colour-Sergeant said.   20
> They are hangin' Danny Deever, you must mark 'im to 'is
> place,
> For 'e shot a comrade sleepin'—you must look 'im in the
> face;
> Nine 'undred of 'is county an' the Regiment's disgrace,
> While they're hangin' Danny Deever in the mornin'.

'What's that so black agin the sun?' said Files-on-Parade.   25
'It's Danny fightin' 'ard for life,' the Colour-Sergeant said.
'What's that that whimpers over'ead?' said Files-on-Parade.
'It's Danny's soul that's passin' now,' the Colour-Sergeant said.
> For they're done with Danny Deever, you can 'ear the
> quickstep play,
> The Regiment's in the column, an' they're marchin' us
> away;   30
> Ho! the young recruits are shakin', an' they'll want their
> beer to-day,
> After hangin' Danny Deever in the mornin'!

Tommy

I went into a public-'ouse to get a pint o' beer,
The publican 'e up an' sez, 'We serve no red-coats here.'
The girls be'ind the bar they laughed an' giggled fit to die,
I outs into the street again an' to myself sez I:
> O it's Tommy this, an' Tommy that, an' 'Tommy, go away'; 5
> But it's 'Thank you, Mister Atkins,' when the band begins to
> play—
> The band begins to play, my boys, the band begins to play,
> O it's 'Thank you, Mister Atkins,' when the band begins to
> play.

I went into a theatre as sober as could be,
They gave a drunk civilian room, but 'adn't none for me;   10
They sent me to the gallery or round the music-'alls,
But when it comes to fightin', Lord! they'll shove me in the stalls!
  For it's Tommy this, an' Tommy that, an' 'Tommy, wait
   outside';
  But it's 'Special train for Atkins' when the trooper's on the
   tide—
  The troopship's on the tide, my boys, the troopship's on the
   tide,   15
  O it's 'Special train for Atkins' when the trooper's on the
   tide.

Yes, makin' mock o' uniforms that guard you while you sleep
Is cheaper than them uniforms, an' they're starvation cheap;
An' hustlin' drunken soldiers when they're goin' large a bit
Is five times better business than paradin' in full kit.   20
  Then it's Tommy this, an' Tommy that, an' 'Tommy, 'ow's
   yer soul?'
  But it's 'Thin red line of 'eroes' when the drums begin to
   roll—
  The drums begin to roll, my boys, the drums begin to roll,
  O it's 'Thin red line of 'eroes' when the drums begin to roll.

We aren't no thin red 'eroes, nor we aren't no blackguards too, 25
But single men in barricks, most remarkable like you;
An' if sometimes our conduck isn't all your fancy paints,
Why, single men in barricks don't grow into plaster saints;
  While it's Tommy this, an' Tommy that, an' 'Tommy, fall
   be'ind,'
  But it's 'Please to walk in front, sir,' when there's trouble in
   the wind—   30
  There's trouble in the wind, my boys, there's trouble in the
   wind,
  O it's 'Please to walk in front, sir,' when there's trouble in
   the wind.

You talk o' better food for us, an' schools, an' fires, an' all:
We'll wait for extry rations if you treat us rational.
Don't mess about the cook-room slops, but prove it to our face 35

The Widow's Uniform is not the soldier-man's disgrace.
    For it's Tommy this, an' Tommy that, an' 'Chuck him out,
        the brute!'
    But it's 'Saviour of 'is country' when the guns begin to
        shoot;
    An' it's Tommy this, an' Tommy that, an' anything you
        please;
    An' Tommy ain't a bloomin' fool—you bet that Tommy
        sees!   40

Fuzzy-Wuzzy

(Soudan Expeditionary Force. Early Campaigns)

We've fought with many men acrost the seas,
An' some of 'em was brave an' some was not;
The Paythan an' the Zulu an' Burmese;
    But the Fuzzy was the finest o' the lot.
We never got a ha'porth's change of 'im: 5
    'E squatted in the scrub an' 'ocked our 'orses,
'E cut our sentries up at Sua*kim*,
    An' 'e played the cat an' banjo with our forces.
        So 'ere's *to* you, Fuzzy-Wuzzy, at your 'ome in the Soudan:
        You're a pore benighted 'eathen but a first-class fightin'
            man;
        We gives you your certificate, an' if you want it signed   11
        We'll come an' 'ave a romp with you whenever you're
            inclined.

We took our chanst among the Kyber 'ills,
    The Boers knocked us silly at a mile,
The Burman give us Irriwaddy chills,   15
    An' a Zulu *impi* dished us up in style:
But all we ever got from such as they
    Was pop to what the Fuzzy made us swaller;
We 'eld our bloomin' own, the papers say,
    But man for man the Fuzzy knocked us 'oller.   20

Then 'ere's *to* you, Fuzzy-Wuzzy, an' the missis and the kid;
Our orders was to break you, an' of course we went an' did.
We sloshed you with Martinis, an' it wasn't 'ardly fair;
But for all the odds agin' you, Fuzzy-Wuz, you broke the
square.

'E ash't got no papers of 'is own,   25
   'E 'asn't got no medals nor rewards,
So *we* must certify the skill 'e's shown
   In usin' of 'is long two-'anded swords:
When 'e's 'oppin' in an' out among the bush
   With 'is coffin-'eaded shield an' shovel-spear,   30
An 'appy day with Fuzzy on the rush
   Will last an 'ealthy Tommy for a year.
      So 'ere's *to* you, Fuzzy-Wuzzy, an' your friends which are no
         more,
      If we 'adn't lost some messmates we would 'elp you to
         deplore.
      But give an' take's the gospel, an' we'll call the bargain
         fair,   35
      For if you 'ave lost more than us, you crumpled up the
         square!

'E rushes at the smoke when we let drive,
   An', before we know, 'e's 'ackin' at our 'ead;
'E's all 'ot sand an' ginger when alive,
   An' 'e's generally shammin' when 'e's dead.   40
'E's a daisy, 'e's a ducky, 'e's a lamb!
   'E's a injia-rubber idiot on the spree,
'E's the on'y thing that doesn't give a damn
   For a Regiment o' British Infantree!
      So 'ere's *to* you, Fuzzy-Wuzzy, at your 'ome in the Soudan;
      You're a pore benighted 'eathen but a first-class fightin'
         man;   46
      An' 'ere's *to* you, Fuzzy-Wuzzy, with your 'ayrick 'ead of
         'air—
      You big black boundin' beggar—for you broke a British
         square!

Gunga Din

You may talk o' gin and beer
When you're quartered safe out 'ere,
An' you're sent to penny-fights an' Aldershot it;
But when it comes to slaughter
You will do your work on water,   5
An' you'll lick the bloomin' boots of 'im that's got it.
Now in Injia's sunny clime,
Where I used to spend my time
A-servin' or 'Er Majesty the Queen,
Of all them blackfaced crew   10
The finest man I knew
Was our regimental bhisti, Gunga Din.
   He was 'Din! Din! Din!
  'You limpin' lump o' brick-dust, Gunga Din!
   'Hi! Slippy *hitherao*!
    'Water, get it! *Panee lao*,[1]   15
  'You squidgy-nosed old idol, Gunga Din.'

The uniform 'e wore
Was nothin' much before,
An' rather less than 'arf o' that be'ind.   20
For a piece o' twisty rag
An' a goatskin water-bag
Was all the field-equipment 'e could find.
When the sweatin' troop-train lay
In a sidin' through the day,   25
Where the 'eat would make your bloomin' eyebrows crawl,
We shouted 'Harry By!'[2]
Till our throats were bricky-dry,
Then we wopped 'im 'cause 'e couldn't serve us all.
   It was 'Din! Din! Din!   30
  'You 'eathen, where the mischief 'ave you been?
   'You put some *juldee*[3] in it

---

[1]   Bring water swiftly.   [2]   O brother.
[3]   Be quick.

'Or I'll *marrow*[1] you this minute
'If you don't fill up my helmet, Gunga Din!'

'E would dot an' carry one   35
Till the longest day was done;
An' 'e didn't seem to know the use o' fear.
If we charged or broke or cut,
You could bet your bloomin' nut,
'E'd be waitin' fifty paces right flank rear.   40
With 'is mussick[2] on 'is back,
'E would skip with our attack,
An' watch us till the bugles made 'Retire,'
An' for all 'is dirty 'ide
'E was white, clear white, inside   45
When 'e went to tend the wounded under fire!
          It was 'Din! Din! Din!'
   With the bullets kickin' dust-spots on the green.
          When the cartridges ran out,
             You could hear the the front-ranks shout,   50
      'Hi! ammunition-mules an' Gunga Din!'

I shan't forgit the night
When I dropped be'ind the fight
With a bullet where my belt-plate should 'a' been.
I was chokin' mad with thirst,   55
An' the man that spied me first
Was our good old grinnin', gruntin' Gunga Din.
'E lifted up my 'ead,
An' he plugged me where I bled,
An' 'e guv me 'arf-a-pint o' water green.   60
It was crawlin' and it stunk,
But of all the drinks I've drunk,
I'm gratefullest to one from Gunga Din.
          It was 'Din! Din! Din!
   ' 'Ere's a beggar with a bullet through 'is spleen;   65
       ' 'E's chawin' up the ground,
       'An' 'e's kickin' all around:
   'For Gawd's sake git the water, Gunga Din!'

---

[1] Hit you.
[2] Water-skin.

'E carried me away
To where a dooli lay,   70
An' a bullet come an' drilled the beggar clean.
'E put me safe inside,
An' just before 'e died,
'I 'ope you liked your drink,' sez Gunga Din.
So I'll meet 'im later on   75
At the place where 'e is gone—
Where it's always double drill and no canteen.
'E'll be squattin' on the coals
Givin' drink to poor damned souls,
An' I'll get a swig in hell from Gunga Din!   80
        Yes, Din! Din! Din!
    You Lazarushian-leather Gunga Din!
        Though I've belted you and flayed you,
        By the livin' Gawd that made you,
        You're a better man than I am, Gunga Din!   85

The Widow at Windsor

'Ave you 'eard o' the Widow at Windsor
With a hairy gold crown on 'er 'ead?
She 'as ships on the foam—she 'as millions at 'ome,
    An' she pays us poor beggars in red.
        (Ow, poor beggars in red!)   5
There's 'er nick on the cavalry 'orses,
        There's 'er mark on the medical stores—
An' 'er troopers you'll find with a fair wind be'ind
    That takes us to various wars.
        (Poor beggars!—barbarious wars!)   10
            Then 'ere's to the Widow at Windsor,
                An' 'ere's to the stores an' the guns,
            The men an' the 'orses what makes up the forces
                O' Missis Victorier's sons
                (Poor beggars! Victorier's sons!)   15

Walk wide o' the Widow at Windsor,
  For 'alf o' Creation she owns:
We 'ave bought 'er the same with the sword an' the flame,
  An' we've salted it down with our bones.
     (Poor beggars!—it's blue with our bones!)   20
Hands off o' the sons o' the Widow,
  Hands off o' the goods in 'er shop,
For the Kings must come down an' the Emperors frown
  When the Widow at Windsor says 'Stop!'
     (Poor beggars!—we're sent to say 'Stop!')   25
       Then 'ere's to the Lodge o' the Widow,
         From the Pole to the Tropics it runs—
         To the Lodge that we tile with the rank an' the file,
         An' open in form with the guns.
     (Poor beggars!—it's always they guns!)   30

We 'ave 'eard o' the Widow at Windsor,
  It's safest to leave 'er alone:
For 'er sentries we stand by the sea an' the land
  Wherever the bugles are blown
     (Poor beggars!—an' don't we get blown!)   35
Take 'old o' the Wings o' the Mornin',
  An' flop round the earth till you're dead;
But you won't get away from the tune that they play
  To the bloomin' old rag over'ead.
     (Poor beggars!—it's 'ot over'ead!)   40
       Then 'ere's to the Sons o' the Widow,
         Wherever, 'owever they roam.
       'Ere's all they desire, an' if they require
         A speedy return to their 'ome.
     (Poor beggars!—they'll never see 'ome!)   45

Mandalay

By the old Moulmein Pagoda, lookin' lazy at the sea,
There's a Burma girl a-settin', and I know she thinks o' me;
For the wind is in the palm-trees, and the temple-bells they say:
'Come you back, you British soldier; come you back to
      Mandalay!'
        Come you back to Mandalay,   5
        Where the old Flotilla lay:
        Can't you 'ear their paddles chunkin' from Rangoon to
          Mandalay?
        On the road to Mandalay,
        Where the flyin'-fishes play,
        An' the dawn comes up like thunder outer China 'crost
          the Bay!   10

'Er petticoat was yaller an' 'er little cap was green,
An' 'er name was Supi-yaw-lat—jes' the same as Theebaw's
      Queen.
An' I seed her first a-smokin' of a whackin' white cheroot,
An' a-wastin' Christian kisses on an 'eathen idol's foot:
        Bloomin' idol made o' mud—   15
        Wot they called the Great Gawd Budd—
        Plucky lot she cared for idols when I kissed 'er where
          she stud!
        On the road to Mandalay . . .

When the mist was on the rice-fields an' the sun was droppin'
      slow,
She'd git 'er little banjo an' she'd sing '*Kulla-lo-lo!*'   20
With 'er arm upon my shoulder an' 'er cheek agin my cheek
We useter watch the steamers an' the *hathis* pilin' teak.
        Elephints a-pilin' teak
        In the sludgy, squdgy creek,
        Where the silence 'ung that 'eavy you was 'arf afraid to
          speak!   25
        On the road to Mandalay . . .

But that's all shove be'ind me—long ago an' fur away,
An' there ain't no 'buses runnin' from the Bank to Mandalay;
An' I'm learnin' 'ere in London what the ten-year soldier tells:
'If you've 'eard the East a-callin', you won't never 'eed naught
    else.'   30
      No! you won't 'eed nothin' else
      But them spicy garlic smells,
      An' the sunshine an' the palm-trees an' the tinkly
        temple-bells;
      On the road to Mandalay . . .

I am sick o' wastin' leather on these gritty pavin'-stones,   35
An' the blasted English drizzle wakes the fever in my bones;
Tho' I walks with fifty 'ousemaids outer Chelsea to the Strand,
An' they talks a lot o' lovin', but wot do they understand?
      Beefy face an' grubby 'and—
      Law! wot do they understand?   40
      I've a neater, sweeter maiden in a cleaner, greener land!
      On the road to Mandalay . . .

Ship me somewheres east of Suez, where the best is like the
    worst,
Where there aren't no Ten Commandments an' a man can raise
    a thirst;
For the temple-bells are callin', an' it's there that I would be— 45
By the old Moulmein Pagoda, looking lazy at the sea;
      On the road to Mandalay,
      Where the old Flotilla lay,
      With our sick beneath the awnings when we went to
        Mandalay!
      O the road to Mandalay,   50
      Where the flyin'-fishes play,
      An' the dawn comes up like thunder outer China 'crost
        the Bay!

The Ladies

I've taken my fun where I've found it;
   I've rogued an' I've ranged in my time;
I've 'ad my pickin o' sweethearts,
   An' four o' the lot was prime.
One was an 'arf-caste widow,   5
   One was a woman at Prome,
One was the wife of a *jemadar-sais*,[1]
   An' one is a girl at 'ome.

Now I aren't no 'and with the ladies,
*   For, takin' 'em all along,*   10
*   You never can say till you've tried 'em,*
*   An' then you are like to be wrong.*
*   There's times when you'll think that you mightn't,*
*   There's times when you'll know that you might;*
*   But the things you will learn from the Yellow an' Brown,* 15
*   They'll 'elp you a lot with the White!*

I was a young un at 'Oogli,
   Shy as a girl to begin;
Aggie de Castrer she made me,
   An' Aggie was clever as sin;   20
Older than me, but my first un—
   More like a mother she were—
Showed me the way to promotion an' pay,
   An' I learned about women from 'er!

Then I was ordered to Burma,   25
   Actin' in charge o' Bazar,
An' I got me a tiddy live 'eathen
   Through buyin supplies off 'er pa.
Funny an' yellow an' faithful—
   Doll in a teacup she were—   30
But we lived on the square, like a true-married pair,
   An' I learned about women from 'er!

[1]   Head-groom.

Then we was shifted to Neemuch
    (Or I might ha' been keepin' 'er now),
An' I took with a shiny she-devil,   35
    The wife of a nigger at Mhow;
'Taught me the gipsy-folks' *bolee*;[1]
    Kind o' volcano she were,
For she knifed me one night 'cause I wished she was white,
    And I learned about women from 'er!   40

Then I come 'ome in a trooper,
    'Long of a kid o' sixteen—
'Girl from a convent at Meerut,
    The straightest I ever 'ave seen.
Love at first sight was 'er trouble,   45
    She didn't know what it were;
An' I wouldn't do such, 'cause I liked 'er too much,
    But—I learned about women from 'er!

I've taken my fun where I've found it,
    An' now I must pay for my fun,   50
For the more you 'ave known o' the others
    The less will you settle to one;
An' the end of it's sittin' and thinkin',
    An' dreamin' Hell-fires to see;
So be warned by my lot (which I know you will not),   55
    An' learn about women from me!

    What did the Colonel's Lady think?
        Nobody never knew.
    Somebody asked the Sergeant's Wife,
        An' she told 'em true!   60
    When you get to a man in the case,
        They're like as a row of pins—
    For the Colonel's Lady an' Judy O'Grady
        Are sisters under their skins!

[1] Slang.

Follow Me 'Ome

There was no one like 'im, 'Orse or Foot,
    Nor any o' the Guns I knew;
An' because it was so, why, o' course 'e went an' died,
    Which is just what the best men do.

    So it's knock out your pipes an' follow me!   5
    An' it's finish up your swipes an' follow me!
      Oh, 'ark to the big drum callin'
        Follow me—follow me 'ome!

'Is mare she neighs the 'ole day long,
    She paws the 'ole night through,   10
An' she won't take 'er feed 'cause o' waitin' for 'is step,
    Which is just what a beast would do.

'Is girl she goes with a bombardier
    Before 'er month is through;
An' the banns are up in church, for she's got the beggar
      hooked,
    Which is just what a girl would do.   16

We fought 'bout a dog—last week it were—
    No more than a round or two;
But I strook 'im cruel 'ard, an' I wish I 'adn't now,
    Which is just what a man can't do.   20

'E was all that I 'ad in the way of a friend,
    An' I've 'ad to find one new;
But I'd give my pay an' stripe for to get the beggar back,
    Which it's just too late to do!

    So it's knock out your pipes an' follow me!   25
    An' it's finish up your swipes an' follow me!
      Oh, 'ark to the fifes a-crawlin'!
        Follow me—follow me 'ome!

Take 'im away! 'E's gone where the best men go.
Take 'im away! An' the gun-wheels turnin' slow. 30
Take 'im away! There's more from the place 'e come.
Take 'im away, with the limber an' the drum.

For it's 'Three rounds blank' an' follow me,
An' it's 'Thirteen rank' an' follow me;
    Oh, passin' the love o' women, 35
      Follow me—follow me 'ome!

Mary, Pity Women!

You call yourself a man,
    For all you used to swear,
An' leave me, as you can,
    My certain shame to bear?
    I 'ear! You do not care— 5
You done the worst you know.
    I 'ate you, grinnin' there . . .
Ah, Gawd, I love you so!

Nice while it lasted, an' now it is over—
Tear out your 'eart an' good-bye to your lover! 10
What's the use o' grievin', when the mother that bore you
(Mary, pity women!) knew it all before you?

    It aren't no false alarm,
      The finish to your fun;
You—you 'ave brung the 'arm, 15
      An' I'm the ruined one!
      An' now you'll off an' run
With some new fool in tow.
      Your 'eart? You 'aven't none . . .
Ah, Gawd, I love you so! 20

When a man is tired there is naught will bind 'im;
All 'e solemn promised 'e will shove be'ind 'im.
What's the good o' prayin' for The Wrath to strike 'im
(Mary, pity women!), when the rest are like 'im?

> What 'ope for me or—it?   25
>   What's left for us to do?
> I've walked with men a bit,
>   But this—but this is you.
>   So 'elp me, Christ, it's true!
> Where can I 'ide or go?   30
>   You coward through and through! . . .
> Ah, Gawd, I love you so!

All the more you give 'em the less are they for givin'—
Love lies dead, an' you cannot kiss 'im livin'.
Down the road 'e led you there is no returnin'   35
(Mary, pity women!), but you're late in learnin'!

> You'd like to treat me fair?
>   You can't, because we're pore?
> We'd starve? What do I care!
>   We might, but *this* is shore!
>   I want the name—no more—   40
> The name, an' lines to show,
>   An' not to be an 'ore. . . .
> Ah, Gawd, I love you so!

What's the good o' pleadin', when the mother that bore you   40
(Mary, pity women!) knew it all before you?
Sleep on 'is promises an' wake to your sorrow
(Mary, pity women!), for we sail to-morrow!

The Absent-Minded Beggar

When you've shouted 'Rule Britannia,' when you've sung 'God
    save the Queen,'
  When you've finished killing Kruger with your mouth,
Will you kindly drop a shilling in my little tambourine
  For a gentleman in khaki ordered South?
He's an absent-minded beggar, and his weaknesses are great— 5
  But we and Paul must take him as we find him—
He is out on active service, wiping something off a slate—
  And he's left a lot of little things behind him!
Duke's son—cook's son—son of a hundred kings—
  (Fifty thousand horse and foot going to Table Bay!)   10
Each of 'em doing his country's work
  (and who's to look after their things?)
Pass the hat for your credit's sake,
             and pay—pay—pay!

There are girls he married secret, asking no permission to, 15
  For he knew he wouldn't get it if he did.
There is gas and coals and vittles, and the house-rent falling due,
  And it's more than rather likely there's a kid.
There are girls he walked with casual. They'll be sorry now he's
    gone,
  For an absent-minded beggar they will find him, 20
But it ain't the time for sermons with the winter coming on.
  We must help the girl that Tommy's left behind him!
Cook's son—Duke's son—son of a belted Earl—
  Son of a Lambeth publican—it's all the same to-day!
Each of 'em doing his country's work 25
  (and who's to look after the girl?)
Pass the hat for your credit's sake,
             and pay—pay—pay!

There are families by thousands, far too proud to beg or speak,
  And they'll put their sticks and bedding up the spout, 30
And they'll live on half o' nothing, paid 'em punctual once a
    week,
  'Cause the man that earns the wage is ordered out.

He's an absent-minded beggar, but he heard his country call,
    And his reg'ment didn't need to send to find him!
He chucked his job and joined it—so the job before us all   35
    Is to help the home that Tommy's left behind him!
Duke's job—cook's job—gardener, baronet, groom,
    Mews or palace or paper-shop, there's someone gone away!
Each of 'em doing his country's work
    (and who's to look after the room?)   40
Pass the hat for your credit's sake,
                  and pay—pay—pay!

Let us manage so as, later, we can look him in the face,
    And tell him—what he'd very much prefer—
That, while he saved the Empire, his employer saved his place,   45
    And his mates (that's you and me) looked out for *her*.
He's an absent-minded beggar and he may forget it all,
    But we do not want his kiddies to remind him
That we sent 'em to the workhouse while their daddy hammered
    Paul,
    So we'll help the homes that Tommy left behind him!   50
Cook's home—Duke's home—home of a millionaire,
    Fifty thousand horse and foot going to Table Bay!)
Each of 'em doing his country's work
    (and what have you got to spare?)
Pass the hat for your credit's sake,   55
                  and pay—pay—pay!

Chant-Pagan

(English Irregular, discharged)

Me that 'ave been what I've been—
Me that 'ave gone where I've gone—
Me that 'ave seen what I've seen—
    'Ow can I ever take on
With awful old England again,   5

An' 'ouses both sides of the street,
And 'edges two sides of the lane,
And the parson an' gentry between,
An' touchin' my 'at when we meet—
    Me that 'ave been what I've been? 10

Me that 'ave watched 'arf a world
'Eave up all shiny with dew,
Kopje on kop to the sun,
An' as soon as the mist let 'em through
Our 'elios winkin' like fun— 15
Three sides of a ninety-mile square,
Over valleys as big as a shire—
'Are ye there? Are ye there? Are ye there?'
An' then the blind drum of our fire . . .
An' I'm rollin' 'is lawns for the Squire, 20
                Me!

Me that 'ave rode through the dark
Forty mile, often, on end,
Along the Ma'ollisberg Range,
With only the stars for my mark 25
An' only the night for my friend,
An' things runnin' off as you pass,
An' things jumpin' up in the grass,
An' the silence, the shine an' the size
Of the 'igh, unexpressible skies— 30
I am takin' some letters almost
As much as a mile to the post,
An' mind you come back with the change!'
                Me!

Me that saw Barberton took 35
When we dropped through the clouds on their 'ead,
An' they 'ove the guns over and fled—
Me that was through Di'mond 'Ill,
An' Pieters an' Springs an' Belfast—
From Dundee to Vereeniging all— 40
Me that stuck out to the last
(An' five bloomin' bars on my chest)—

I am doin' my Sunday-school best,
By the 'elp of the Squire an' 'is wife
(Not to mention the 'ousemaid an' cook),   45
To come in an' 'ands up an' be still,
An' honestly work for my bread,
My livin' in that state of life
To which it shall please God to call
                                        Me!   50

Me that 'ave followed my trade
In the place where the Lightnin's are made;
'Twixt the Rains and the Sun and the Moon—
Me that lay down an' got up
Three years with the sky for my roof—   55
That 'ave ridden my 'unger an' thirst
Six thousand raw mile on the hoof,
With the Vaal and the Orange for cup,
An' the Brandwater Basin for dish,—
Oh! it's 'ard to be'ave as they wish   60
(Too 'ard, an' a little too soon),
I'll 'ave to think over it first—
                                        Me!

I will arise an' get 'ence—
I will trek South and make sure   65
If it's only my fancy or not
That the sunshine of England is pale,
And the breezes of England are stale,
An' there's somethin' gone small with the lot.
For *I* know of a sun an' a wind,   70
An' some plains and a mountain be'ind,
An' some graves by a barb-wire fence,
An' a Dutchman I've fought 'oo might give
Me a job were I ever inclined
To look in an' offsaddle an' live   75
Where there's neither a road nor a tree—
But only my Maker an' me,
And I think it will kill me or cure,
So I think I will go there an' see.
                                        Me!   80

Puck's Song

(Enlarged from 'Puck of Pook's Hill')

See you the ferny ride that steals
Into the oak-woods far?
O that was whence they hewed the keels
That rolled to Trafalgar.

And mark you where the ivy clings   5
To Bayham's mouldering walls?
O there we cast the stout railings
That stand around St. Paul's.

See you the dimpled track that runs
All hollow through the wheat?   10
O that was where they hauled the guns
That smote King Philip's fleet.

(Out of the Weald, the secret Weald,
Men sent in ancient years
The horse-shoes red at Flodden Field,   15
The arrows at Poitiers!)

See you our little mill that clacks,
So busy by the brook?
She has ground her corn and paid her tax
Ever since Domesday Book.   20

See you our stilly woods of oak,
And the dread ditch beside?
O that was where the Saxons broke
On the day that Harold died.

See you the windy levels spread   25
About the gates of Rye?
O that was where the Northmen fled,
When Alfred's ships came by.

See you our pastures wide and lone,
Where the red oxen browse?   30

O there was a City thronged and known,
Ere London boasted a house.

And see you, after rain, the trace
Of mound and ditch and wall?
O that was a Legion's camping-place,   35
When Cæsar sailed from Gaul.

And see you marks that show and fade,
Like shadows on the Downs?
O they are the lines the Flint Men made,
To guard their wondrous towns.   40

Trackway and Camp and City lost,
Salt Marsh where now is corn—
Old Wars, old Peace, old Arts that cease,
And so was England born!

She is not any common Earth,   45
Water or wood or air,
But Merlin's Isle of Gramarye,
Where you and I will fare!

The Way Through The Woods

('Marklake Witches'—*Rewards and Fairies*)

They shut the road through the woods
Seventy years ago.
Weather and rain have undone it again,
And now you would never know
There was once a road through the woods   5
Before they planted the trees.
It is underneath the coppice and heath
And the thin anemones.
Only the keeper sees

That, where the ring-dove broods,   10
And the badgers roll at ease,
There was once a road through the woods.

Yet, if you enter the woods
Of a summer evening late,
When the night-air cools on the trout-ringed pools   15
Where the otter whistles his mate,
(They fear not men in the woods,
Because they see so few.)
You will hear the beat of a horse's feet,
And the swish of a skirt in the dew,   20
Steadily cantering through
The misty solitudes,
As though they perfectly knew
The old lost road through the woods . . . .
But there is no road through the woods.   25

A Tree Song

(AD 1200)
('Weland's Sword'—*Puck of Pook's Hill*)

Of all the trees that grow so fair,
    Old England to adorn,
Greater are none beneath the Sun
    Than Oak, and Ash, and Thorn.
Sing Oak, and Ash, and Thorn, good sirs,   5
    (All of a Midsummer morn!)
Surely we sing no little thing
    In Oak, and Ash, and Thorn!

Oak of the Clay lived many a day
    Or ever Æneas began.   10
Ash of the Loam was a lady at home
    When Brut was an outlaw man.
Thorn of the Down saw New Troy Town

(From which was London born);
Witness hereby the ancientry   15
    Of Oak, and Ash, and Thorn!

Yew that is old in churchyard-mould,
    He breedeth a mighty bow.
Alder for shoes do wise men choose,   20
    And beech for cups also.
But when ye have killed, and your bowl is spilled,
    And your shoes are clean outworn,
Back ye must speed for all that ye need
    To Oak, and Ash, and Thorn!

Ellum she hateth mankind, and waiteth   25
    Till every gust be laid
To drop a limb on the head of him
    That anyway trusts her shade.
But whether a lad be sober or sad,
    Or mellow with ale from the horn,   30
He will take no wrong when he lieth along
    'Neath Oak, and Ash, and Thorn!

Oh, do not tell the Priest our plight,
    Or he would call it a sin;
But—we have been out in the woods all night,   35
    A-conjuring Summer in!
And we bring you news by word of mouth—
    Good news for cattle and corn—
Now is the Sun come up from the South
    With Oak, and Ash, and Thorn!   40

Sing Oak, and Ash, and Thorn, good sirs
    (All of a Midsummer morn)!
England shall bide, till Judgment Tide
    By Oak, and Ash, and Thorn!

A Charm

(*Introduction to 'Rewards and Fairies'*)

Take of English earth as much
As either hand may rightly clutch.
In the taking of it breathe
Prayer for all who lie beneath.
Not the great nor well-bespoke,   5
But the mere uncounted folk
Of whose life and death is none
Report or lamentation.
　　Lay that earth upon thy heart,
　　And thy sickness shall depart!   10

It shall sweeten and make whole
Fevered breath and festered soul.
It shall mightily restrain
Over-busied hand and brain.
It shall ease thy mortal strife   15
'Gainst the immortal woe of life,
Till thyself, restored, shall prove
By what grace the Heavens do move.

Take of English flowers these—
Spring's full-facèd primroses,   20
Summer's wild wide-hearted rose,
Autumn's wall-flower of the close,
And, thy darkness to illume,
Winter's bee-thronged ivy-bloom.
Seek and serve them where they bide   25
From Candlemas to Christmas-tide,
　　For these simples, used aright,
　　Can restore a failing sight.

These shall cleanse and purify
Webbed and inward-turning eye;   30
These shall show thee treasure hid
Thy familiar fields amid;

And reveal (which is thy need)
Every man a King indeed!

Eddi's Service

(AD 687)
('The Conversion of St. Wilfrid'—
Rewards and Fairies)

Eddi, priest of St Wilfrid
   In his chapel at Manhood End,
Ordered a midnight service
   For such as cared to attend.

But the Saxons were keeping Christmas,   5
   And the night was stormy as well.
Nobody came to service,
   Though Eddi rang the bell.

' 'Wicked weather for walking,'
   Said Eddi of Manhood End.   10
'But I must go on with the service
   For such as care to attend.'

The altar-lamps were lighted,—
   An old marsh-donkey came,
Bold as a guest invited,   15
   And stared at the guttering flame.

The storm beat on at the windows,
   The water splashed on the floor,
And a wet, yoke-weary bullock
   Pushed in through the open door.   20

'How do I know what is greatest,
   How do I know what is least?

That is My Father's business,'
  Said Eddi, Wilfrid's priest.

'But—three are gathered together—   25
  Listen to me and attend.
I bring good news, my brethren!'
  Ould Eddi of Manhood End.

And he told the Ox of a Manger
  And a Stall in Bethlehem,   30
And he spoke to the Ass of a Rider
  That rode to Jerusalem.

They steamed and dripped in the chancel,
  They listened and never stirred,
While, just as though they were Bishops,   35
  Eddi preached them The Word,

Till the gale blew off on the marshes
  And the windows showed the day,
And the Ox and the Ass together
  Wheeled and clattered away.   40

And when the Saxons mocked him,
  Said Eddi of Manhood End,
'I dare not shut His chapel
  On such as care to attend.'

Harp Song of the Dane Women

  ('The Knights of the Joyous Venture'—
    Puck of Pook's Hill)

What is a woman that you forsake her,
And the hearth-fire and the home-acre,
To go with the old grey Widow-maker?

She has no house to lay a guest in—
But one chill bed for all to rest in,   5
That the pale suns and the stray bergs nest in.

She has no strong white arms to fold you,
But the ten-times-fingering weed to hold you—
Out on the rocks where the tide has rolled you.

Yet, when the signs of summer thicken,   10
And the ice breaks, and the birch-buds quicken,
Yearly you turn from our side, and sicken—

Sicken again for the shouts and the slaughters.
You steal away to the lapping waters,
And look at your ship in her winter-quarters.

You forget our mirth, and talk at the tables,
The kine in the shed and the horse in the stables—
To pitch her sides and go over her cables.

Then you drive out where the storm-clouds swallow,
And the sound of your oar-blades, falling hollow,   20
Is all we have left through the months to follow.

Ah, what is Woman that you forsake her,
And the hearth-fire and the home-acre,
To go with the old grey Widow-maker?

A St Helena Lullaby

('A Priest in spite of Himself'—*Rewards and Fairies*)

'How far is St Helena from a little child at play?'
What makes you want to wander there with all the
            world between?
Oh, Mother, call your son again or else he'll run away.
(*No one thinks of winter when the grass is green!*)

'How far is St Helena from a fight in Paris Street?'   5
I haven't time to answer now—the men are falling fast.
The guns begin to thunder, and the drums begin to beat.
(*If you take the first step, you will take the last!*)

'How far is St Helena from the field of Austerlitz?'
You couldn't hear me if I told—so loud the cannon roar,   10
But not so far for people who are living by their wits.
('*Gay go up*' means '*Gay go down*' the wide world o'er!)

'How far is St. Helena from an Emperor of France?'
I cannot see—I cannot tell—the Crowns they dazzle so.
The Kings sit down to dinner, and the Queens stand up
     to dance.   15
(*After open weather you may look for snow!*)

'How far is St. Helena from the Capes of Trafalgar?'
A longish way—a longish way—with ten year more to run.
It's South across the water underneath a falling star.
(*What you cannot finish you must leave undone!*)   20

'How far is St. Helena from the Beresina ice?'
An ill way—a chill way—the ice begins to crack.
But not so far for gentlemen who never took advice.
(*When you can't go forward you must e'en come back!*)

'How far is St. Helena from the field of Waterloo?'   25
A near way—a clear way—the ship will take you soon.
A pleasant place for gentlemen with little left to do.
(*Morning never tries you till the afternoon!*)

'How far from St. Helena to the Gate of Heaven's Grace?'
That no one knows—that no one knows—and no one ever will.30
But fold your hands across your heart and cover up your face,
And after all your trapesings, child, lie still!

Road-Song of the *Bandar-Log*

('Kaa's Hunting'—*The Jungle Book*)

Here we go in a flung festoon,
Half-way up to the jealous moon!
Don't you envy our pranceful bands?
Don't you wish you had extra hands?
Wouldn't you like if your tails were—*so*—   5
Curved in the shape of a Cupid's bow?
    Now you're angry, but—never mind,
    Brother, thy tail hangs down behind!

Here we sit in a branchy row,
Thinking of beautiful things we know;   10
Dreaming of deeds that we mean to do,
All complete, in a minute or two—
Something noble and grand and good,
Won by merely wishing we could.
    Now we're going to—never mind,   15
    Brother, thy tail hangs down behind!

All the talk we ever have heard
Uttered by bat or beast or bird—
Hide or fin or scale or feather—
Jabber it quickly and all together!   20
Excellent! Wonderful! Once again!
Now we are talking just like men.
    Let's pretend we are . . . Never mind!
    Brother, thy tail hangs down behind!
    This is the way of the Monkey-kind!   25

Then join our leaping lines that scumfish through the pines,
That rocket by where, light and high, the wild-grape swings.
By the rubbish in our wake, and the noble noise we make,
Be sure—be sure, we're going to do some splendid things!

The Law of the Jungle

('How Fear Came'—*The Second Jungle Book*)

Now this is the Law of the Jungle—as old and as true as the sky;
And the Wolf that shall keep it may prosper, but the Wolf that shall
break it must die.

As the creeper that girdles the tree-trunk the Law runneth forward and
    back—
For the strength of the Pack is the Wolf, and the strength of the Wolf
    is the Pack.

Wash daily from nose-tip to tail-tip; drink deeply, but never too
    deep;   5
And remember the night is for hunting, and forget not the day is
    for sleep.

The Jackal may follow the Tiger, but, Cub, when thy whiskers are
    grown,
Remember the Wolf is a hunter—go forth and get food of thine
    own.

Keep peace with the Lords of the Jungle—the Tiger, the Panther,
    the Bear;
And trouble not Hathi the Silent, and mock not the Boar in his
    lair.   10

When Pack meets with Pack in the Jungle, and neither will go
    from the trail,
Lie down till the leaders have spoken—it may be fair words shall
    prevail.

When ye fight with a Wolf of the Pack, ye must fight him alone
    and afar,
Lest others take part in the quarrel, and the Pack be diminished
    by war.

The Lair of the Wolf is his refuge, and where he has made him his
    home,   15

Not even the Head Wolf may enter, not even the Council may
    come.

The Lair of the Wolf is his refuge, but where he has digged it too
    plain,
The Council shall send him a message, and so he shall change it
    again.

If ye kill before midnight, be silent, and wake not the woods with
    your bay,
Lest ye frighten the deer from the crops, and the brothers go
    empty away.   20

Ye may kill for yourselves, and your mates, and your cubs as
    they need, and ye can;
But kill not for pleasure of killing, and *seven times never kill Man!*

If ye plunder his Kill from a weaker, devour not all in thy pride;
Pack-Right is the right of the meanest; so leave him the head and
    the hide.

The Kill of the Pack is the meat of the Pack. Ye must eat where it
    lies;   25
And no one may carry away of that meat to his lair, or he dies.

The Kill of the Wolf is the meat of the Wolf. He may do what he
    will,
But, till he has given permission, the Pack may not eat of that
    Kill.

Cub-Right is the right of the Yearling. From all of his Pack he
    may claim
Full-gorge when the killer has eaten; and none may refuse him
    the same.   30

Lair-Right is the right of the Mother. From all of her year she may
    claim
One haunch of each kill for her litter; and none may deny her the
    same.

Cave-Right is the right of the Father—to hunt by himself for his
    own:
He is freed of all calls to the Pack; he is judged by the Council
    alone.

Because of his age and his cunning, because of his gripe and his
    paw,   35
In all that the Law leaveth open, the word of the Head Wolf is
    Law.

Now these are the Laws of the Jungle, and many and mighty are they;
But the head and the hoof of the Law and the haunch and the hump
    - is—Obey!

If——

('Brother Square-Toes'—*Rewards and Fairies*)

If you can keep your head when all about you
    Are losing theirs and blaming it on you,
If you can trust yourself when all men doubt you,
    But make allowance for their doubting too;
If you can wait and not be tired by waiting,   5
    Or being lied about, don't deal in lies,
Or being hated, don't give way to hating,
    And yet don't look too good, nor talk too wise:

If you can dream—and not make dreams your master;
    If you can think—and not make thoughts your aim;   10
If you can meet with Triumph and Disaster
    And treat those two imposters just the same;
If you can bear to hear the truth you've spoken
    Twisted by knaves to make a trap for fools,
Or watch the things you gave your life to, broken,   15
    And stoop and build 'em up with worn-out tools:

If you can make one heap of all your winnings
   And risk it on one turn of pitch-and-toss,
And lose, and start again at your beginnings
   And never breathe a word about your loss;   20
If you can force your heart and nerve and sinew
   To serve your turn long after they are gone,
And so hold on when there is nothing in you
   Except the Will which says to them: 'Hold on!'

If you can talk with crowds and keep your virtue,   25
   Or walk with Kings—nor lose the common touch,
If neither foes nor loving friends can hurt you,
   If all men count with you, but none too much;
If you can fill the unforgiving minute
   With sixty seconds' worth of distance run,   30
Yours is the Earth and everything that's in it,
   And—which is more—you'll be a Man, my son!

The Land

('Friendly Brook'—*A Diversity of Creatures*)

When Julius Fabricius, Sub-Prefect of the Weald,
In the days of Diocletian owned our Lower River-field,
He called to him Hobdenius—a Briton of the Clay,
Saying: 'What about the River-piece for layin' in to hay?'

And the aged Hobden answered: 'I remember as a lad   5
My father told your father that she wanted dreenin' bad.
An' the more that you neeglect her the less you'll get her clean.
Have it jest *as* you've a mind to, but, if I was you, I'd dreen.'

So they drained it long and crossways in the lavish Roman
       style—
Still we find among the river-drift their flakes of ancient tile,   10
And in drouthy middle August, when the bones of meadows
       show,

We can trace the lines they followed sixteen hundred years ago.

Then Julius Fabricius died as even Prefects do,
And after certain centuries, Imperial Rome died too.
Then did robbers enter Britain from across the Northern main   15
And our Lower River-field was won by Ogier the Dane.

Well could Ogier work his war-boat—well could Ogier wield his
　　　　brand—
Much he knew of foaming waters—not so much of farming land.
So he called to him a Hobden of the old unaltered blood,　　　19
Saying: 'What about that River-piece; she doesn't look no good?'

And that aged Hobden answered: ' 'Tain't for *me* to interfere,
But I've known that bit o' meadow now for five and fifty year.
Have it *jest* as you've a mind to, but I've proved it time on time,
If you want to change her nature you have *got* to give her lime!'

Ogier sent his wains to Lewes, twenty hours' solemn walk,　　25
And drew back great abundance of the cool, grey, healing chalk.
And old Hobden spread it broadcast, never heeding what was
　　　　in't.—
Which is why in cleaning ditches, now and then we find a flint.

Ogier died. His sons grew English—Anglo-Saxon was their
　　　　name—
Till out of blossomed Normandy another pirate came;　　　30
For Duke William conquered England and divided with his men,
And our Lower River-field he gave to William of Warenne.

But the Brook (you know her habit) rose one rainy autumn night
And tore down sodden flitches of the bank to left and right.
So, said William to his Bailiff as they rode their dripping rounds:35
'Hob, what about that River-bit—the Brook's got up no bounds?'

And that aged Hobden answered: ' 'Tain't my business to advise,
But ye might ha' known 'twould happen from the way the valley
　　　　lies.
Where ye can't hold back the water you must try and save the
　　　　sile.

Hev it jest as you've a *mind* to, but, if I was you, I'd spile!' 40

They spiled along the water-course with trunks of willow-trees,
And planks of elms behind 'em and immortal oaken knees.
And when the spates of Autumn whirl the gravel-beds away
You can see their faithful fragments, iron-hard in iron clay.

*

Georgii Quinti Anno Sexto, I, who own the River-field, 45
Am fortified with title-deeds, attested, signed and sealed,
Guaranteeing me, my assigns, my executors and heirs
All sorts of powers and profits which—are neither mine nor
       theirs.

I have rights of chase and warren, as my dignity requires.
I can fish—but Hobden tickles. I can shoot—but Hobden wires. 50
I repair, but he reopens, certain gaps which, men allege,
Have been used by every Hobden since a Hobden swapped a
       hedge.

Shall I dog his morning progress o'er the track-betraying dew?
Demand his dinner-basket into which my pheasant flew?
Confiscate his evening faggot under which my conies ran, 55
And summons him to judgment? I would sooner summons Pan.

His dead are in the churchyard—thirty generations laid.
Their names were old in history when Domesday Book was
       made;
And the passion and the piety and prowess of his line
Have seeded, rooted, fruited in some land the Law calls mine. 60

Not for any beast that burrows, not for any bird that flies,
Would I lose his large sound counsel, miss his keen amending
       eyes.
He is bailiff, woodman, wheelwright, field-surveyor, engineer,
And if flagrantly a poacher—'tain't for me to interfere.

'Hob, what about that River-bit?' I turn to him again, 65

With Fabricius and Ogier and William of Warenne.
'Hev it jest as you've a mind to, *but*'—and here he takes
    command.
For whoever pays the taxes old Mus' Hobden owns the land.

The Song of the Little Hunter

('The King's Ankus'—*The Second Jungle Book*)

Ere Mor the Peacock flutters, ere the Monkey People cry,
    Ere Chil the Kite swoops down a furlong sheer,
Through the Jungle very softly flits a shadow and a sigh—
    He is Fear, O Little Hunter, he is Fear!
Very softly down the glade runs a waiting, watching shade,   5
    And the whisper spreads and widens far and near.
And the sweat is on thy brow, for he passes even now—
    He is Fear, O Little Hunter, he is Fear!

Ere the moon has climbed the mountain, ere the rocks are ribbed
    with light,
    When the downward-dipping trails are dank and drear,   10
Comes a breathing hard behind thee—*snuffle-snuffle* through the
    night—
    It is Fear, O Little Hunter, it is Fear!
On thy knees and draw the bow; bid the shrilling arrow go;
    In the empty, mocking thicket plunge the spear!
But thy hands are loosed and weak, and the blood has left thy
    cheek—   15
    It is Fear, O Little Hunter, it is Fear!

When the heat-cloud sucks the tempest, when the slivered pine-
    trees fall,
    When the blinding, blaring rain-squalls lash and veer,
Through the war-gongs of the thunder rings a voice more loud
    than all—
    It is Fear, O Little Hunter, it is Fear!   20
Now the spates are banked and deep; now the footless boulders
    leap—

Now the lightning shows each littlest leaf-rib clear—
But thy throat is shut and dried, and thy heart against thy side
   Hammers: Fear, O Little Hunter—this is Fear!

The Secret of the Machines

(MODERN MACHINERY)

We were taken from the ore-bed and the mine,
   We were melted in the furnace and the pit—
We were cast and wrought and hammered to design,
   We were cut and filed and tooled and gauged to fit.
Some water, coal, and oil is all we ask,   5
   And a thousandth of an inch to give us play:
And now, if you will set us to our task,
   We will serve you four and twenty hours a day!

   We can pull and haul and push and lift and drive,
      We can print and plough and weave and heat and light,   10
   We can run and race and swim and fly and dive,
      We can see and hear and count and read and write!

Would you call a friend from half across the world?
   If you'll let us have his name and town and state,
You shall see and hear your crackling question hurled   15
   Across the arch of heaven while you wait.
Has he answered? Does he need you at his side?
   You can start this very evening if you choose,
And take the Western Ocean in the stride
   Of seventy thousand horses and some screws!   20

   The boat-express is waiting your command!
      You will find the *Mauretania* at the quay,
   Till her captain turns the lever 'neath his hand,
      And the monstrous nine-decked city goes to sea.

Do you wish to make the mountains bare their head 25
    And lay their new-cut forests at your feet?
Do you want to turn a river in its bed,
    Or plant a barren wilderness with wheat?
Shall we pipe aloft and bring you water down
    From the never-failing cisterns of the snows, 30
To work the mills and tramways in your town,
    And irrigate your orchards as it flows?

    It is easy! Give us dynamite and drills!
    Watch the iron-shouldered rocks lie down and quake,
    As the thirsty desert-level floods and fills, 35
    And the valley we have dammed becomes a lake.

But remember, please, the Law by which we live,
    We are not built to comprehend a lie,
We can neither love nor pity nor forgive.
    If you make a slip in handling us you die! 40
We are greater than the Peoples or the Kings—
    Be humble, as you crawl beneath our rods!—
Our touch can alter all created things,
    We are everything on earth—except The Gods!

    Though our smoke may hide the Heavens from your eyes, 45
    It will vanish and the stars will shine again,
    Because, for all our power and weight and size,
    We are nothing more than children of your brain!

The Storm Cone

This is the midnight—let no star
Delude us—dawn is very far.
This is the tempest long foretold—
Slow to make head but sure to hold.

Stand by! The lull 'twixt blast and blast   5
Signals the storm is near, not past;
And worse than present jeopardy
May our forlorn to-morrow be.

If we have cleared the expectant reef,
Let no man look for his relief.   10
Only the darkness hides the shape
Of further peril to escape.

It is decreed that we abide
The weight of gale against the tide
And those huge waves the outer main   15
Sends in to set us back again.

They fall and whelm. We strain to hear
The pulses of her labouring gear,
Till the deep throb beneath us proves,
After each shudder and check, she moves!   20

She moves, with all save purpose lost,
To make her offing from the coast;
But, till she fetches open sea,
Let no man deem that he is free!

The Appeal

IF I HAVE GIVEN YOU DELIGHT
  BY AUGHT THAT I HAVE DONE,
LET ME LIE QUIET IN THAT NIGHT
  WHICH SHALL BE YOURS ANON:

AND FOR THE LITTLE, LITTLE SPAN
  THE DEAD ARE BORNE IN MIND,
SEEK NOT TO QUESTION OTHER THAN
  THE BOOKS I LEAVE BEHIND.

Notes

The poems in this selection are chosen from *Rudyard Kipling's Verse: Definitive Edition* (London: Hodder and Stoughton 1940, 1973), which follows the format prepared by Kipling for the Sussex Edition of *Verse, Inclusive Edition 1885–1932*, though with additional material supplied by his daughter. It is not a chronological arrangement, but the first collection in which each poem appears is given in brackets after the title.

The Post that Fitted (*Departmental Ditties*, 1886).
15 modus operandi: way of operating, a plan of action. **16 Pears's shaving sticks:** 'Pears' soap products used popular images of purity in their advertising campaigns.

Sestina of the Tramp-Royal (*The Seven Seas*, 1896)
Sestina: a poem of six-line stanzas, with an envoi, which uses the same line endings in different orders in each stanza. The use of this consciously artificial form contrasts with the language, rhythms and practicalities of its speaker. **17 tucker** Australian slang for the daily rations of a gold-digger or station hand. Hence, food, grub.

The Explorer (*The Five Nations*, 1903)
17 Norther: strong, cold, north wind. **25 aloes:** plant with bitter purgative juices. Figuratively, bitter experiences. **27 dwined:** wasted or dwindled away. **43 Saul he went to look for donkeys:** 1 Samuel 9:3. After searching for his father's asses, Saul asks directions from the prophet Samuel and is appointed 'captain over my people Israel' by him.

McAndrew's Hymn (*The Seven Seas*, 1896)
5 John Calvin: Jean Calvin, French Protestant reformer whose theological doctrines emphasized predetermined election, the predestination of the saved and those condemned to hellfire. **6 Institutio:** statement of Protestant belief as in Calvin's *Institutio Christianae Religionis* (1536). **52 blind-fou:** blind mad, raging. **66 fetich:** fetish. **119 ross ...:** rossignol. **130 Apollyon:** Greek name for the destroying angel. See Revelations 9:11. **177 Man – the Artifex!:** man, the artificer.

185 Pelagian: from Palagius, latinised name of Jerome, who denied the doctrine of Original Sin.

The *Mary Gloster* (*The Seven Seas*, 1896)
19 Grub that 'ud bind you crazy: food that would make you constipated.

The Liner she's a Lady (*The Seven Seas*, 1896)
5 Jenny: As in Rossetti's poem, a popular name for a fallen woman.

My Boy Jack (*Destroyers at Jutland; Sea Warfare*, both 1916)
Kipling's son John, a subaltern with the Irish Guards, was killed in action at the Battle of Loos, 1915. The Battle of Jutland was fought in the North Sea in May and June 1916.

The Vampire (*Verse, Inclusive Edition*, 1919)
Written in 1897 to accompany the exhibition catalogue entry for Philip Burne-Jones' painting of a modern vampire (Philip Burne-Jones was Kipling's cousin). Bram Stoker's *Dracula* was published later in the same year.

The English Flag (*Barrack Room Ballads*, 1892)
The report from the 'Daily Papers' which precedes the poem concerns a demonstration during a trial of Irish political agitators at Cork in 1891, where the court-house was set on fire. **23 sea-egg:** sea urchin. **29 halliards:** ropes or tackle for raising and lowering sails. **43 Hoogli:** Hooghly, the river on which Calcutta stands.

The Ballad of East and West (*Barrack Room Ballads*, 1892)
8 calkins: the turned down ends of horseshoes. **11 Ressaldar:** native captain in an Indian cavalry regiment.

Gehazi (*The Years Between*, 1919)
The parable of Elisha and Gehazi (2 Kings 5) is used here to comment on the Marconi Affair of 1912 where the acceptance of the Marconi company's tender for a proposed Imperial wireless chain sparked off rumours that cabinet ministers, including Sir Rufus Isaacs – the Gehazi of the poem – had corruptly influenced the bargain in order to profit from its soaring shares. The enquiry excited further controversy by implicating other ministers, including Lloyd George. The House was divided over the

ministers' protestations of good faith, though in the end their regrets were accepted on a party vote. **1 Whence comest thou, Gehazi: 2** Kings 5:25. **44 A leper white as snow:** 2 Kings 5:27.

The Islanders (*The Five Nations,* 1903)
Written in the wake of the losses of the Boer War, this poem emphasizes Kipling's conviction that Britain should be armed and prepared for future conflicts. **1 No doubt but ye are the people:** Job 12:3. **47 As it were almost cricket:** cf. Henry Newbolt's 'Vita Lampada' for the cricket/war analogy. **67 gelt:** gelded, emasculated. **76 Baals:** false gods. **77 Teraphs of sept and party:** tribal gods or idols.

The White Man's Burden (*The Five Nations* 1903)
After a short war with Spain in 1898, America took over the administration of the Philippines and Cuba. As it was a leading anti-Imperialist country until this time, the poem celebrates America's change of direction. **40 Our loved Egyptian Night:** refers to the Israelites' reluctance to follow Moses and Aaron to the Promised Land. See Exodus 16:2,3.

Recessional (*The Five Nations,* 1903)
Imperial self-confidence, so much a part of the Golden Jubilee ten years before, was more muted by 1897 at Victoria's Diamond Jubilee celebrations, for which this poem was written. By the 1890s there was increasing unease about expansionism and aggression, however the poem still surprised both admirers and detractors with the solemnity of its warnings. A Recessional is a hymn sung while the clergy and choir are retiring from a church service. **16 Nineveh and Tyre:** past empires, fallen to invaders. **22 Or lesser breeds without the Law:** a much debated line. See Romans 2:10–14.

The Three Decker (*The Seven Seas,* 1896)
In 1894, the system of publishing novels in three volumes (popularly known as three-deckers) collapsed, fundamentally changing the style and nature of prose fiction. **4 Islands of the Blest:** In Greek myth the Hesperides, containing the gardens where the fabled golden apples grow. **9 Cook:** Thomas Cook, travel agent. **16 Yussuf ... Zuleika:** 'Yussuf' was the pen-name under which 'The Ballad of East and West' first appeared in 1889 and is another name for Joseph (also Kipling's first name). Zuleika is thought to be the name of Potiphar's wife, who tempted

Joseph. See Genesis 39. **35 Flying Dutchman:** a spectral ship supposedly seen off the Cape of Good Hope. **35 from truck to taffrail dressed:** the truck is at the top of the mast, the taffrail is the aftermost portion of the poop deck, hence, flags flown along the full length of the halliards.

The Conundrum of the Workshops (*Barrack Room Ballads*, 1892)
2 Tree: of the knowledge of Good and Evil (Genesis 2:9). **8 Cain:** son of Adam and Eve who murdered his brother Abel (Genesis 4). **9 a tower:** the Tower of Babel (Genesis 11). **14 the waters:** of the Flood (Genesis 7). **21 surplice-peg:** tent peg. **22 yelk:** yolk. **29 Four Great Rivers:** the four rivers which came to a head to water the Garden of Eden (Genesis 2: 10–14)

The Benefactors (*The Years Between*, 1919).

When 'Omer Smote 'is Bloomin' Lyre (*The Seven Seas*, 1896).
The introduction to the Barrack Room Ballads section of *The Seven Seas*.
1 'Omer: Homer, poet of the great classical epics, *Iliad* and *Odyssey*.

Tomlinson (*Barrack Room Ballads*, 1892)
85 Empusa's crew: hobgoblins.

The Female of the Species (*The Years Between*, 1919).
Written in response to militant suffragist action in 1911. **9 Hurons and Choctaws:** native American tribes.

The Sons of Martha (*The Years Between*, 1919).
1 Mary: the mother of Christ who is privileged and sanctified.
2 Martha: the woman who works and serves others.

Danny Deever (*Barrack Room Ballads*, 1892).
1 Files-on- Parade: ordinary soldier(s). **2 Colour-Sergeant:** army sergeant who attends to the regimental colours on ceremonial occasions.

Tommy (*Barrack Room Ballads*, 1892).
· Tommy Atkins is the generic name for the typical private soldier. Already in use, it was further popularised by this poem. **14 trooper:** ship for carrying soldiers overseas. **22 'thin red line of 'eroes':** phrase used originally of the 93rd Highlanders at Balaclava in 1854. **36 Widow's Uniform:** the 'Widow' refers to Victoria, hence a soldier of the Queen.

'**Fuzzy-Wuzzy**' (*Barrack Room Ballads*, 1892)
The nickname was given to the warriors of Eastern Sudanese tribes who wore their long hair frizzed out. **7 Suakim:** Suakin, south of Port Sudan on the Red Sea. **13 chanst:** chance. **16 impi:** a regiment of Zulu warriors, one almost wiped out the British at Isandlhwana in 1879. **19 the papers say:** British public sentiment in 1884 was against Gordon's plan to commission Zebeir Pasha to hold Khartoum and the Nile valley against the Mahdi. The cabinet yielded to this force of opinion, making it a factor in the chain of events which led to Gordon's death at Khartoum. **24 the square:** military formation. The Baggara tribe of the western Sudan broke into a square of 1500 British infantry at Abu Klea, 1884.

Gunga Din (*Barrack Room Ballads*, 1892)
A dramatic recitation based on a true story which occurred at the siege of Delhi in 1857. **3 penny fights and Aldershot it:** skirmishes and training campaigns (Aldershot being an army training camp in Hampshire). **12 bhisti:** native water-carrier. **15–16 hitherao panee lao:** bring water, quickly. **27 Harry-by:** O brother. **32 juldee:** be quick. **33 marrow:** hit. **41 mussick:** water-skin, leather carrier. **70 dooli:** stretcher.

The Widow at Windsor (*Barrack Room Ballads*, 1892)
1 Widow: Queen Victoria. **2 hairy:** perhaps a euphemism for 'bloody'. **4 beggars:** euphemism for 'buggers'. **6 nick:** the Queen's mark of an upwardly pointing arrow. **28 Lodge that we tile:** Masonic allusions; a Lodge is a masonic 'workshop' and to 'tile' it is to defend it. **36 Wings o' the Morning:** Psalms 139:9.

Mandalay (*Barrack Room Ballads*, 1892).
This much-loved poem was written to a popular waltz tune. **12 Supi-yaw-lat . . . Theebaw's Queen:** Queen Supaya-lat and King Theebaw of Upper Burma, driven to exile in 1885. **16 Great God Budd:** Great God Buddha. **22 hathis:** elephants.

The Ladies (*The Seven Seas*, 1896).
6 Prome: is in Burma. **7 jemadar-sais:** a head groom. **17 'Oogli:** Hooghly, a suburb of Calcutta named after the river. **26 Actin' in charge o' Bazar:** acting as sergeant in charge of the regimental store

and canteen. **33 Neemuch:** Nimach in Rajasthan, India. **36 Mhow:** in Central India. **37 bolee:** gypsy slang. **43 Meerut:** near Delhi, India.

Follow Me 'Ome (*The Seven Seas*, 1896).
1–2 no one like 'im, 'Orse or Foot, Nor any o' the Guns I knew: from the old army phrase 'Horse, Foot and Guns'. **6 swipes:** poor quality beer, and the act of drinking it in one draught. **29–32:** this stanza composed to Handel's 'Dead March'. **35 passin' the love o' women:** David's lament for Jonathon, 2 Samuel 1:26.

Mary, Pity Women! (*The Seven Seas*, 1896)
A monologue or music-hall recitation in the sentimental 'My Man' mode, this ballad was one of those which influenced Bertolt Brecht.

The Absent-Minded Beggar (*Inclusive Edition*, 1919).
This poem was published in the *Daily Mail* in 1899, and then circulated in a variety of forms to raise funds for the families of soldiers serving in the Boer War. Set to music, it was sung in the music-halls and raised over £250,000 for family aid. **6 Paul:** Paul Kruger, president of the Transvaal Republic and leader of the Boers. **8 wiping something off a slate:** reversing the losses of the first Boer War in 1880. **10 Table Bay:** the harbour of Cape Town. **30 put their sticks and bedding up the spout:** pawn their furniture and bedding.

Chant-Pagan (*The Five Nations*, 1903)
13 kopje on kop: kopje (pron. koppy) is a hill; kop is a mountain. **15 'elios:** heliographs, instruments for communicating using the sun's rays. **24 Ma'ollisberg Range:** the Magaliesberg range of mountains near Johannesberg, a stronghold of the guerrilla leader General de la Rey. **38 Di'mond 'ill:** scene of Roberts' defeat of Botha. **39 Pieters an' Springs an' Belfast:** various scenes of action in Natal and the Transvaal. **40 Dundee to Vereeniging:** Dundee saw some of the first fighting in Northern Natal; Vereeninging, near Pretoria, is the place where the Boers surrendered. The Peace of Vereeniging, signed on 31 May 1902 brought the Boer War to a close.

Puck's Song (*Songs from Books*, 1913)
In its initial form appeared in *Puck of Pook's Hill* (1906). **4 Trafalgar:** scene of Nelson's defeat of the French and Spanish navies in 1805. **12 King Philip's fleet:** Spanish Armada, defeated by the British in

1588. **15 Flodden Field:** battlefield in North Northumberland where the English defeated the Scots under James IV in 1513. **16 Potiers:** where Edward, the Black Prince, defeated John II of France in 1356. **24 the day that Harold died:** he was shot through the eye at the Battle of Hastings in 1066 and succeeded by William of Normandy (William the Conqueror). **47 Merlin's Isle of Gramarye:** aligns the island of the Arthurian enchanter with the magic of art and words (through the primary and secondary connotations of 'Gramarye': 'grammar' and 'occult learning').

The Way through the Woods (*Songs from Books*, 1913)
First appeared in *Rewards and Fairies*, 1910.

A Tree Song (*Songs from Books*, 1913) .
First appeared in *Puck of Pook's Hill*, 1906. **10 Aeneas:** hero of Virgil's epic, the *Aeneid*. **12 Brut:** the Trojan Brutus, reputed first king and founder of Britain. A 'Brutus' is also a name for a hero in a British, Welsh or Arthurian story.

A Charm (*Songs from Books*, 1913)
Introductory poem to *Rewards and Fairies* (1910), though two lines were dropped for this version of the text for the *Definitive Edition*. **26 Candlemas:** Feast of the Purification of the Virgin Mary, 2 February. **27 simples:** plants or herbs used for medicinal purposes.

Eddi's Service (*Songs from Books* 1913)
First appeared in *Rewards and Fairies*, 1910. **1 St Wilfrid:** patron saint of Sussex.

Harp Song of the Dane Women (*Songs from Books*, 1913)
First appeared in *Puck of Pook's Hill*, 1906.

A St Helena Lullaby (*Songs from Books*, 1913)
First appeared in *Rewards and Fairies*, 1910. **1 St Helena:** island of Napoleon Bonaparte's exile, where he died in 1821. **5 fight in Paris Street:** refers to the French Revolution. **9 Austerlitz:** in Moravia, scene of celebrated Napoleonic victory against the Austro-Hungarian forces. **12 'Gay go up' means 'Gay go down':** from the nursery rhyme 'The Bells of London Town'. **13 an Emperor of France:** in 1804 Napoleon induced the Pope to come to Paris for his coronation but at the last

moment placed the crown on his own head. **17 the Capes of Trafalgar:** where the English navy annihilated the combined body of the French and Spanish fleets in 1805. **21 the Beresina ice:** frozen river crossing where a minor skirmish took place on Napoleon's retreat from Moscow. **25 Waterloo:** place in Belgium of Napoleon's final defeat in 1815, which preceded his exile in St Helena. **32 trapesings:** aimless wanderings.

Road-Song of the Bandar-Log (*Songs from Books*, 1913)
First appeared in the *Jungle Book*, 1894. The bandar-log are monkeys who exist outside the 'Law'. They are aligned with movement, change and flux – are fun-loving and untrustworthy. **26 scumfish:** verb which juxtaposes their movements through the trees with the scum that floats on the surface of the water.

The Law of the Jungle (*Songs from Books*, 1913)
First appeared in the *Second Jungle Book*, 1895.

If—— (*Songs from Books*, 1913)
First appeared in *Rewards and Fairies*, 1910.

The Land (*Songs for Youth*, 1924)
First appeared in *A Diversity of Creatures*, 1917. **2 Diocletian:** Roman Emperor who abdicated AD 305. **6 dreenin':** draining. **25 wains:** carts. **31 Duke William:** William of Normandy (William the Conqueror). **40 spile:** to shore up with wooden stakes or plugs. **45 Georgii Quinti Anno Sexto:** the sixth year of George V. **55 faggot . . . conies:** firewood, rabbits.

The Song of the Little Hunter (*Songs from Books*, 1913).
First appeared in the *Second Jungle Book*, 1895.

The Secret of the Machines (*Twenty Poems*, 1918)
First appeared in *A History of England*, 1911. **22 Mauretania:** transatlantic passenger ship of the Cunard line. Launched in 1906 with a maiden voyage in 1907, she was known as the 'Grand Old Lady of the Atlantic'.

The Storm Cone (*Inclusive Edition*, 1933)
A storm cone is a black cone hoisted by coastguards to warn of

approaching storms. **6 the storm is near, not past:** Kipling felt that
the threat from Germany had not been allayed by the ending of the Great
War.

The Appeal (*Definitive Edition*, 1940)

Everyman's Poetry

Titles available in this series

William Blake
ed. Peter Butter
0 460 87800 X

The Brontës
ed. Pamela Norris
0 460 87864 6

**Rupert Brooke &
Wilfred Owen**
ed. George Walter
0 460 87801 8

**Elizabeth Barrett
Browning**
ed. Colin Graham
0 460 87894 8

Robert Browning
ed. Colin Graham
0 460 87893 X

Robert Burns
ed. Donald Low
0 460 87814 X

Lord Byron
ed. Jane Stabler
0 460 87810 7

Geoffrey Chaucer:
Comic and Bawdy Tales
ed. Malcolm Andrew
0 460 87869 7

John Clare
ed. R. K. R. Thornton
0 460 87823 9

Arthur Hugh Clough
ed. John Beer
0 460 87939 1

Samuel Taylor Coleridge
ed. John Beer
0 460 87826 3

Dante
ed. Anna Lawrence
0 460 87955 3

Emily Dickinson
ed. Helen McNeil
0 460 87895 6

John Donne
ed. D. J. Enright
0 460 87901 4

John Dryden
ed. David Hopkins
0 460 87940 5

Four Metaphysical Poets
ed. Douglas Brooks-Davies
0 460 87857 3

Oliver Goldsmith
ed Robert L. Mack
0 460 87827 1

Thomas Gray
ed. Robert L. Mack
0 460 87805 0

Ivor Gurney
ed. George Walter
0 460 87797 6

Thomas Hardy
ed. Norman Page
0 460 87956 1

Heinrich Heine
ed. T. J. Reed
& David Cram
0 460 87865 4

George Herbert
ed. D. J. Enright
0 460 87795 X

Robert Herrick
ed. Douglas Brooks-Davies
0 460 87799 2

John Keats
ed. Nicholas Roe
0 460 87808 5

Omar Khayyám
ed. Tony Briggs
0 460 87954 5

Rudyard Kipling
ed. Jan Hewitt
0 460 87941 3

**Henry Wadsworth
Longfellow**
ed. Anthony Thwaite
0 460 87821 2